PAUL'S LIFE AND LETTERS

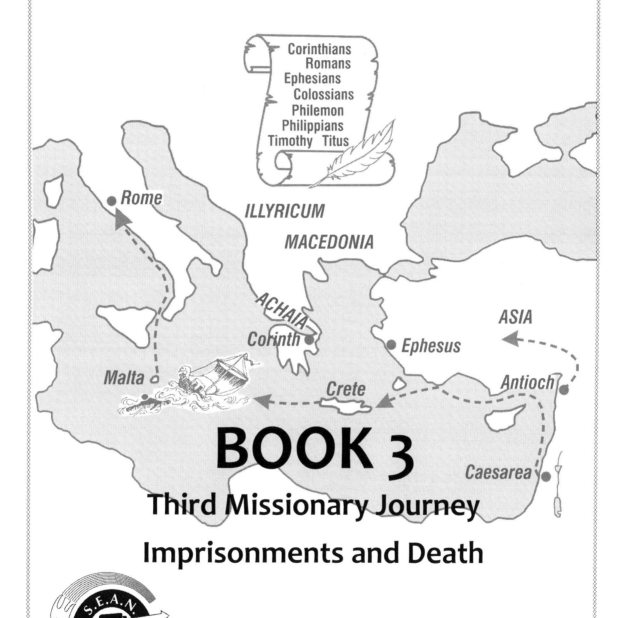

Corinthians
Romans
Ephesians
Colossians
Philemon
Philippians
Timothy Titus

Rome

ILLYRICUM

MACEDONIA

ACHAIA

Corinth

ASIA

Ephesus

Malta

Crete

Antioch

Caesarea

BOOK 3

Third Missionary Journey

Imprisonments and Death

S.E.A.N.
2 TIMOTHY 2:2
STUDY BY EXTENSION FOR ALL NATIONS

Student Workbook

SEAN International

SEAN (pronounced "Say-an") means Study by Extension for All Nations.

Paul's Life and Letters – Book 3 is the third of a series of three books which teach the themes of Paul's letters and present his life and missionary journeys in detail.

Each are intended to be studied in a group directed by a Group Leader who uses the accompanying Group Leader's Guide.

This SEAN course has been based on the New International Version of the Bible. If you use other versions, adjustments may be necessary.

Our website:
www.seaninternational.org

Our e-mail:
contact@seaninternational.org

First English Edition 1990
New Revised American English Edition 2021
(Updated 2023)
ISBN: 978-1-899049-72-1

SEAN International is a UK Registered Charity (No. 286965).

Cover image: ID 51181154 © Tetyana Kochneva | Dreamstime.com

Contents

Introduction

This Book is the third in a series of three on "Paul's Life and Letters". The whole series is as follows.

Book 1 Paul's birth, early life, and first missionary journey, with his letter to the Galatians.

Book 2 The second missionary journey and the related letters, especially 1 and 2 Thessalonians.

Book 3 The third missionary journey, imprisonments and martyrdom, and related letters.

Objectives of Book 3

On completing Book 3 of this Course each student will be able to achieve the following:

a) Describe the main events that took place in Ephesus, naming Paul's closest colleagues and the part that each played in building up Christ's church in Asia. Name two of the opponents to the gospel in Ephesus and say what they did.

b) Name the three ways in which Paul caused the gospel to spread throughout the whole of Asia. Name at least two of the Asian churches that came into being and the people associated with them. Give examples of Paul's teaching in the letters he wrote to the Asian Christians. Name one letter that has been lost which he wrote to an Asian church.

c) Outline the main points in Paul's ministry to Corinth while he was based in Ephesus. Explain his purpose in writing each of his four letters to them and say where he was on each occasion. Explain why Paul made the quick journey from Ephesus to Corinth, that is not mentioned in Acts.

d) Explain the vital part that Titus played in this ministry to Corinth.

e) Say what plans Paul made for his future while he was in Ephesus and how these were fulfilled in a way very different from what he had thought.

f) Give passages from Paul's letters that throw light on a period of intense anguish through which he passed during his last days in Ephesus. Give the spiritual lessons Paul drew from these sufferings.

g) Name the two very important letters that Paul wrote when he revisited Macedonia and Achaia and the places where he wrote them. Give some of the relevant facts and spiritual truths that we can learn from them.

h) Give events that happened in Troas, Miletus and Caesarea on the return journey to Jerusalem.

i) Give the principal events that led up to, or took place on, Paul's journey as a prisoner to Rome, with special emphasis on what happened in Jerusalem, Caesarea, Crete, Malta and Rome itself. Say what this journey teaches us about Paul's walk with Christ.

j) Give examples of the places Paul must have visited in the period between his imprisonments; name the two people to whom he wrote letters at this time, say where these people were and what we can learn about their respective ministries for Christ from the letters.

k) Describe the circumstances of Paul's final imprisonment and death. Name the letter he wrote at this time and show from this how Paul faced death.

l) On the Test Map, locate 16 of the main places associated with this period in Paul's life and give an important event that took place in each.

m) Put Paul's letters from this period in the probable order in which they were written and give the main purpose for writing each of them.

Instructions on How to Do the Lessons

1. **Lessons A, B** and **C** are to be completed at home by the students.

2. **Lessons C** are Group Bible Studies which will be reviewed in the weekly Group Meetings with the Group Leader and the rest of the students.

How to Use the Lessons for Research and Review

Research Instructions

1. As in Books 1 and 2, blank lines are provided for you to write the answers to each numbered point. You can find the answers by looking up the place in the Bible or elsewhere as indicated in the reference at the end of the line.

2. You can, if you prefer, write the answers in a notebook with their numbering as given in the lesson, e.g. 1a) 1b) etc. In this way you will be able to review better.

3. After completing each numbered point, check (and if necessary correct) your answer(s) for that number. You will find the correct answers at the foot of the page. The answers to Lessons C are in the Group Leader's Guide and will be checked at the Group Meeting.

Remember:

First: Find the answer by looking up the reference, or by working it out.
Second: Write your answers in the blanks provided, or if you prefer, in a notebook.
Third: Complete each point before checking and then go on to the next one.

Review Instructions

4. Do the lesson once and then review by going through it again, making sure you have understood and learned the whole lesson well.

5. Once you are confident that you have mastered the contents you should do the test for the corresponding lesson. You will find these tests, starting on page 136 of this workbook.

6. Then, finally do Lesson C, but not the test which you will do at home after the Group Meeting.

Introductory Group Study
Summary of the Mission to Asia

Welcome to Book 3 on Paul's life and letters. This Book majors on Paul's third missionary journey, and the rest of his life, with the related letters. This Bible study reviews the history of the churches in Asia from the time Paul labored there, up to the time John wrote Revelation to them.

Note: *This was the Roman province of Asia, much smaller than the continent of Asia today.*

1. The main thrust of Paul's **third** missionary journey was to **Asia based on Ephesus**; and what a mission it was!

    a) Read, for example, Acts 19:10 and 26. How many heard the word of the Lord during Paul's two year mission to Asia?

    _____

    _____

    b) The large number of important passages and books in the New Testament that are connected in some way with Asia, and especially the city of Ephesus, also show the impact of Paul's mission there. Most of these are listed in Supplement 3 on page 134.

    Glance at these now, and say which is the
    passage that deals with Paul's two year mission to Asia.   _____

2. Before going on, perhaps we should just glance at Items 1 and 2 in Supplement 3, which give us the events leading up to Paul's mission there. Which are these? Those of you who have done Book 2 should remember them.

    1) _____

    _____

    2) _____

    _____

    _____

3. Once the mission to Asia (the **third** journey) was over, Paul revisited the churches in Macedonia and Achaia that he had planted on his earlier **second** journey, before finally returning home by sea. On this homeward voyage the ship docked near Ephesus giving Paul the chance to meet the Christians once again as is recorded in Acts 20.

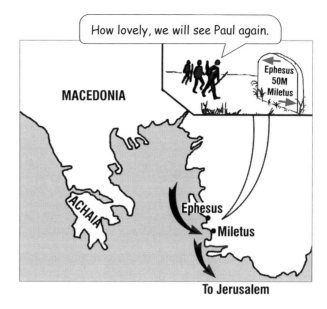

Look carefully at the map before continuing.

a) Read Acts 20:17–18 and after comparing it with the map say how, where, and with whom, this meeting took place.

_____

_____

_____

b) Read Acts 20:31–35. In his farewell speech, what does Paul say about the way he had behaved when he was previously in Ephesus?

_____

_____

_____

c) Read Acts 20:28–30. What did Paul foresee would happen in the church in Ephesus in the future?

_____

_____

_____

d) Using Supplement 3, find the complete passage that deals with this farewell speech to the Christians from Ephesus. (Leader: make sure **all** students have found this before continuing.)

_____

4. We can trace the history of the churches in Asia in the New Testament right up to the time when, years later, John the apostle was imprisoned on the lonely island of Patmos for his faith in Jesus, and from there wrote Revelation to the churches in Asia (Rev. 1:9). To how many churches in Asia did he write? (See map opposite and Revelation 1:4.)

_____

_____

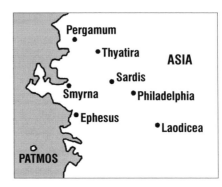

✐ **Note 1:** Make sure that everyone understands that this map is an **enlarged** view of the tiny area around Ephesus (A) and Colossae (G) on the Test Map on page 155. In this way we have zoomed in on all these places (rather as if we were looking at it in greater detail through a magnifying glass).

✐ **Note 2:** You can read the messages John wrote to each of these churches in Revelation 2:1 to 3:22.

✐ **Note 3:** There is some doubt as to the identity of the John who wrote Revelation. We follow the strongly attested traditional belief that it was the apostle John.

5. Let's look briefly at what John wrote to one of these 7 churches in Asia — Ephesus. After seeing Paul's earlier fears, that he had expressed in his farewell speech to the Ephesian elders, perhaps it should not surprise us to see what John has to say to them here years later. Read what he says in Revelation 2:1–7.

    a) What does John tell us here, that shows us how Paul's earlier fears, expressed in his farewell speech to the Ephesian elders (Acts 20:28–30), had unhappily come to pass?

    _____

    _____

    _____

    b) What effect did this seem to have had on the church in Ephesus, both for good and for evil?

    _____

    _____

    c) What did John urge them to do?

    _____

6. Finally, from Supplement 3, you can see that Paul wrote **seven** of his New Testament letters either from or to Asia, or about things that happened there. Which are these letters?

    _____

    _____

    Let's look at some of the things he taught about love in his letter to the **Ephesians** which give us a glimpse of the kind of love the Ephesians had learned about from Paul.

Paul's Teaching about Love in Ephesians

7. Read Ephesians 1:15–16; 3:17–19; 4:2–3 and 15–16; 5:2; 6:23–24.

    Describe some of the features of love as seen in these verses, e.g. its source, its objects and its different ways of expression.

    _____

    _____

    _____

8. **To Think and Pray About**

Now let's ask the Lord to help us to put this kind of love into practice in our own lives.

9. **Next Week**

Please do Lessons 1A and 1B (with their **Tests**), then do Lesson 1C in preparation for next week's Group Meeting. In these Paul arrives in Ephesus and starts his ministry in Asia.

Lesson 1A

The Third Missionary Journey

Outward Bound (Acts 18:18–28)

In this lesson we will see how
A. Paul **approaches** Ephesus via **Galatia**, as
B. Apollos **leaves** Ephesus for **Corinth**.

1. Which of the maps below shows

    a) Paul's journey?   Map _____

    b) Apollos' journey?   Map _____

A
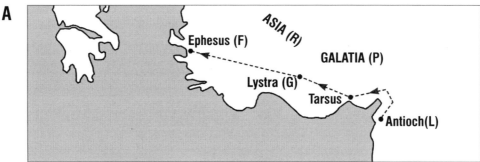

B
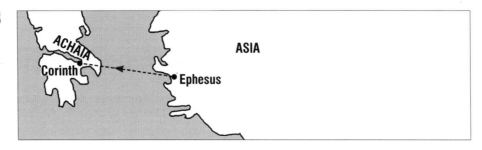

At long last we come to Paul's **third** missionary journey which was to Ephesus (Asia), but first we must refresh our memory on the events that led up to this.

Answers

1. a) Map A
   b) Map B

---

2. **Review**

You may remember how on Paul's homeward journey from his second missionary journey he had made a flying visit to the important Asian city of a) _____ (Acts 18:19) where he had left behind his two colleagues b) _____ and c) _____ (Acts 18:19; in Supplement 3 this is listed as Item 2).

Once back in Antioch Paul gave a full report to this church that had sent him out on his second journey.

However, it wasn't long before Paul was restless to get back again to the couple he had left in Asia, so he set off on his d) _____ missionary journey. In the Acts, Luke continues the story.

A. Paul Approaches Ephesus Via Galatia

3. Read Acts 18:23. (**Note:** In numbers 3 to 5 use Map "A" on the previous page.)

Yes, Paul was anxious to get to Aquila and Priscilla whom he had left in the city of a) _____ in the province of b) _____. On his way out by land he visited again the churches he had established on his **first** missionary journey, in the province of c) _____ (Acts 18:23), marked on Map "A" by the letter d) _____.

4. As we saw in Book 2, one of Paul's chief concerns on his **third** missionary journey was to raise money for the poor in Judea; that is his "Aid to Jerusalem" project. So he didn't let any grass grow under his feet but immediately asked the churches in a) _____ (1 Cor. 16:1) if they would help! Remember it was here that Paul had enlisted for his missionary team the young man called b) _____ (Acts 16:1–3) on his c) _____ missionary journey. Now they were glad to help again.

5. It must have been a great thrill for Timothy to get back to his home town of a) _____, marked on Map "A" by the letter b) _____, and to hear all the latest news. Soon, however, they left Galatia and made straight for the city of c) _____ (Acts 19:1), marked on Map "A" by the letter d) _____, situated in the province of e) _____, marked on Map "A" by the letter f) _____.

6. So Paul visited Galatia on **each** of his 3 missionary journeys. Let's remind ourselves of what happened on each occasion, by looking at the following pictures.

✎ **Note:** Throughout this course Paul is always dressed in clothes shaded with dots, so that you can recognize him easily.

Answers

2. a) Ephesus	3. a) Ephesus	5. a) Lystra
b) Priscilla	b) Asia	b) G
c) Aquila	c) Galatia	c) Ephesus
d) third	d) P	d) F
	4. a) Galatia	e) Asia
	b) Timothy	f) R
	c) second	

Lystra in Galatia

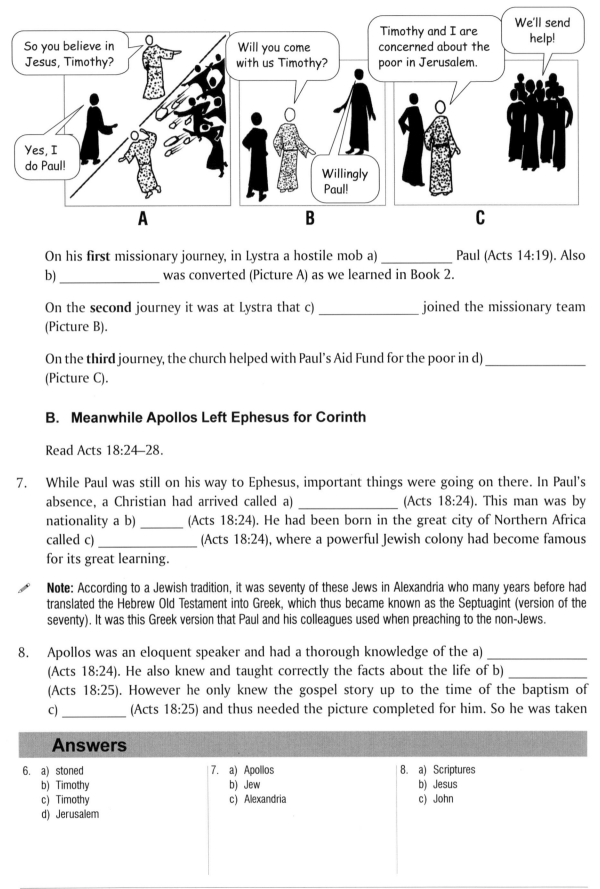

On his **first** missionary journey, in Lystra a hostile mob a) _____ Paul (Acts 14:19). Also b) _____ was converted (Picture A) as we learned in Book 2.

On the **second** journey it was at Lystra that c) _____ joined the missionary team (Picture B).

On the **third** journey, the church helped with Paul's Aid Fund for the poor in d) _____ (Picture C).

B. Meanwhile Apollos Left Ephesus for Corinth

Read Acts 18:24–28.

7. While Paul was still on his way to Ephesus, important things were going on there. In Paul's absence, a Christian had arrived called a) _____ (Acts 18:24). This man was by nationality a b) _____ (Acts 18:24). He had been born in the great city of Northern Africa called c) _____ (Acts 18:24), where a powerful Jewish colony had become famous for its great learning.

🖊 **Note:** According to a Jewish tradition, it was seventy of these Jews in Alexandria who many years before had translated the Hebrew Old Testament into Greek, which thus became known as the Septuagint (version of the seventy). It was this Greek version that Paul and his colleagues used when preaching to the non-Jews.

8. Apollos was an eloquent speaker and had a thorough knowledge of the a) _____ (Acts 18:24). He also knew and taught correctly the facts about the life of b) _____ (Acts 18:25). However he only knew the gospel story up to the time of the baptism of c) _____ (Acts 18:25) and thus needed the picture completed for him. So he was taken

Answers

6.	a) stoned	7.	a) Apollos	8.	a) Scriptures
	b) Timothy		b) Jew		b) Jesus
	c) Timothy		c) Alexandria		c) John
	d) Jerusalem				

under the wing of d) _____ and e) _____ (Acts 18:26) who taught him more correctly the Way of God. (In Supplement 3, this is listed under Item 3.)

9. After this, Apollos decided to go and visit the church in the city of a) _____ (Acts 18:27 with 19:1). So the believers in b) _____ (Acts 18:27), presumably impressed by his preaching, decided to send a c) _____ of recommendation (Acts 18:27) to the church there. On arriving, Apollos was a great help to the Christians. He confounded the unbelieving Jews with his strong arguments from the Scriptures that Jesus was indeed the d) _____ (Acts 18:28).

10. However this visit was not without its problems. Not long after, it led to serious a) _____ (1 Cor. 1:10) in the church, and one of the groups that Paul had to rebuke had in effect begun to idolize the Alexandrian Jew named b) _____. (1 Cor. 1:12)

11. Now look at the pictures below, which summarize these events in Apollos' life.

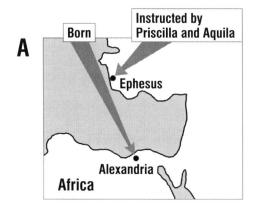 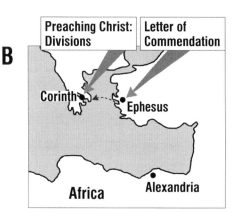

Picture A shows us that Apollos was born in a) _____ a city in Northern b) _____. Then, as a Christian he moved to the city of c) _____ where he was instructed more correctly by d) _____ and e) _____.

Picture B shows us that Apollos (just before Paul's arrival) left f) _____ carrying with him a g) _____ of h) _____ to the church in i) _____. Here he preached faithfully about j) _____, but unhappily his presence there led to k) _____ in the church.

12. So when Paul finally arrived back in a) _____, having traveled through Galatia and the interior of the province of Asia, Apollos was already in b) _____ (Acts 19:1).

Answers

8. d) Priscilla
   e) Aquila
9. a) Corinth
   b) Ephesus
   c) letter
   d) Messiah
10. a) division

10. b) Apollos
11. a) Alexandria
    b) Africa
    c) Ephesus
    d) Priscilla
    e) Aquila
    f) Ephesus

11. g) letter
    h) recommendation
    i) Corinth
    j) Jesus
    k) divisions
12. a) Ephesus
    b) Corinth

13. At last the Lord led Paul to Asia, the province he had so wanted to visit on his **second** journey but had not done so on his way out because he had been stopped by the _____ _____ (Acts 16:6). (In Supplement 3, this is listed in Item 1.)

14. Because Paul had been obedient on that occasion, and had **not** gone into Asia, he had been able to establish **four** new, vigorous churches in Europe instead. These were (revision of Book 2):

Churches		**Province**	
a) _____ (Acts 16:12)			
b) _____ (Acts 17:1)		d) _____ (Acts 16:12)	
c) _____ (Acts 17:10)			
e) _____ (Acts 18:1)		f) _____ (Acts 18:12)	

But Now Was God's Time for Paul to Go into Asia

To Think and Pray About

Paul had wanted to launch his mission to Asia at the beginning of his **second** journey. Clearly this was

1) in God's plan, but

2) **not** in God's time.

Now, however, God's time had arrived. Read Paul's account of the blessings he saw in the lives of the Ephesians as a result — in Ephesians 2:1, 13, 20–22. Sometimes we get fretful at delays in what we are convinced is God's programme for us, instead of patiently waiting for God's time. However, it is better to take a detour **with** God than a shortcut **without** him! How does Jesus' example in John 11:6 and 43–45 illustrate this same principle? God's **delays** do not necessarily mean his **disapproval**. Does this apply to any plans you may have at the moment, and what can you learn from it?

15. Now review, as instructed in Points 4 and 5 on page 3. Then when you feel confident, do Test 1A on page 136.

Answers

13. Holy Spirit
14. a) Philippi
    b) Thessalonica
    c) Berea

14. d) Macedonia
    e) Corinth
    f) Achaia

Lesson 1B

Ephesus at Last

(Acts 19:1–7)

> In this lesson we will see how Paul arrived in Ephesus and got involved in the following activities:
> a)   Teaching (both in public and in private)
> b)   A mini-Pentecost (with speaking in other tongues)
> c)   Tent making again

1.   Which Picture (A, B or C) from this or the next page, illustrates each of the titles given above.

Title a)   Picture _____

Title b)   Picture _____

Title c)   Picture _____

Yes Priscilla, it's just like the old days in <u>Corinth</u> again. (Acts 18:1-3)

Thank you dear Paul for this gift, fruit of your toil. (Acts 20:35)

Aquila! how lovely to be back at tentmaking now we are in <u>Ephesus</u>. (Acts 20:33-35; 1 Cor. 4:12)

A

Even in <u>Thessalonica</u> I earned my living this way. (2 Thess. 3:7-8)

Answers

1.   a) Picture B
     b) Picture C
     c) Picture A

B

C

2. Read Acts 19:1–7

    Now at last Paul was able to achieve his long ambition to witness for Christ in the province of Asia. Having passed through the interior of the province he headed straight for the coastal city of a) _____ (Acts 19:1) which was to become his base for the next b) _____ years (Acts 20:31). Check its position again on Map "A" in Lesson 1A.1. Remember how we saw in our last lesson (Map "B") that when Paul arrived here, Apollos had already moved on to c) _____ (Acts 19:1). Remember, too, that we are now studying Paul's d) _____ missionary journey.

3. **Review**

    Let's just go over the provinces where Paul set up **new** churches on each of his missionary journeys.

    First journey in the province of a) G_____ .

    Second journey in the provinces of b) M_____ and c) A_____ .

    Third journey in the province of d) A_____ .

    ✎ **Note:** These were the new provinces where his main ministry was carried out on each journey. On each subsequent journey he always revisited the churches he had set up on previous journeys as well.

4. The first thing that would have caught Paul's eye in Ephesus, even in a city full of dazzling white buildings, would have been the mighty temple of the goddess a) _____ (Acts 19:24, 35). The cult of this goddess held sway over the city of b) _____ (Acts 19:28) and throughout the whole province of c) _____ (Acts 19:27).

    ✎ **Note:** "Artemis" is called "Diana" in some Bibles.

5. From what Paul said later in his farewell talk with the elders of the church in Ephesus we can learn that he did the same here as he had done previously in Thessalonica and Corinth on his second missionary journey; that is, he began immediately to a) _____ with his b) _____ (Acts 20:34) to provide not only for himself, but also for his c) _____ (Acts 20:34). Not only this, but he also earned sufficient to help the d) _____ (Acts 20:35). In this way he did not have to take from the people of Ephesus either e) _____ or f) _____ or g) _____ (Acts 20:33). This we can see in Picture h) _____ (at the beginning of this lesson).

6. Of course Paul would have used his trade as a maker of a) _____ (Acts 18:3) and have gone into partnership again with the Christian couple who had accompanied him from Corinth, that is b) _____ and c) _____ (Acts 18:19), who had already established themselves in their trade of making d) _____ (Acts 18:3) in the city of e) _____ (Acts 18:19) during Paul's absence in Jerusalem and Antioch.

Answers

2. a) Ephesus	3. a) Galatia	5. a) work	6. a) tents
b) three	b) Macedonia	b) hands	b) Priscilla
c) Corinth	c) Achaia	c) companions	c) Aquila
d) third	d) Asia	d) weak	d) tents
	4. a) Artemis	e) silver	e) Ephesus
	b) Ephesus	f) gold	
	c) Asia	g) clothing	
		h) A	

7. From the farewell talk with the Ephesian elders we also see what Paul taught while he was in Ephesus, that is the a) _____ _____ of God (Acts 20:27). This he did both b) _____ and in their c) _____ (Acts 20:20). This we see illustrated in Picture d) ____.

8. What a man Paul was, tirelessly working for his living and teaching God's word publicly and from house to house. Busy in this way and soon after arriving in Ephesus, Paul bumped into a small group of believers; they were in number about a) _____ (Acts 19:7). In chatting together Paul soon found that they only knew about the baptism of b) _____ (Acts 19:3). In this they were like c) _____ (Acts 18:24–25) before he had been better instructed by d) _____ and e) _____ (Acts 18:26).

9. But perhaps even worse, these believers had never heard about the a) _____ _____ (Acts 19:2). So after explaining all this to them, Paul baptized them in the name of b) _____ (Acts 19:5) and then, after Paul had laid his c) _____ (Acts 19:6) on them, the d) _____ _____ (Acts 19:6) came upon them and they spoke in e) _____ (Acts 19:6) and f) _____ (Acts 19:6), as we see in Picture g) ____.

10. This was a kind of mini-Pentecost and it is interesting to see how years later, when Paul wrote to Ephesus, he still emphasized the importance of the Holy Spirit. *"Do not"* he said, *"a) _____ the Holy Spirit of God"* (Eph. 4:30). *"Instead, be b) _____* (Eph. 5:18) *with the c) _____"* (Eph. 5:18).

Note: In the Group Study on the letter to the Ephesians we will see more of what Paul taught them about the Holy Spirit.

11. **To Think and Pray About**

    As an introduction to this teaching in Ephesians on the Holy Spirit read Ephesians 6:17–18. According to these verses, in what two areas can the Spirit help us in our studies?

    a) _____ b) _____.

    Why not ask for his help now?

12. **Now review and do Test 1B.**

    Then do Lesson 1C, but leave the test until after the Group Meeting.

Answers

7. a) whole will
    b) publicly
    c) homes
    d) B
8. a) twelve
    b) John
    c) Apollos

8. d) Priscilla
    e) Aquila
9. a) Holy Spirit
    b) Jesus
    c) hands
    d) Holy Spirit
    e) tongues

9. f) prophesied
    g) C
10. a) grieve
    b) filled
    c) Spirit
11. a) The word of God
    b) prayer

Lesson 1C
Group Study

The Presence and Power of the Holy Spirit
(Paul's Letter to the Ephesians)

> *In this Group Study we will be looking at:*
> *A. Paul's Spirit-filled ministry in Ephesus*
> *B. Paul's teaching on the Holy Spirit in Ephesians*
>
> *Paul's letter, called "to the Ephesians", was probably meant to be circulated among several of the churches in Asia, rather like John's "Revelation". It was probably written from Rome toward the end of Paul's life; nevertheless, it also helps us to understand better the things that happened during his time of ministry in Ephesus. What Paul says about the Holy Spirit in Ephesians was, of course, a subject that would have been especially meaningful to a church that started with a mini-Pentecost, as we saw in the last lesson.*

A. Paul's Spirit-Filled Ministry in Ephesus

1. **Review**

   As we saw in Lesson 1B, no sooner had Paul arrived in Ephesus than he met a group of believers who had not heard about the Holy Spirit. Paul baptized them and placed his hands upon them.

   What three things happened then? (Acts 19:6)

   a) _____

   b) _____

   c) _____

   So these believers experienced the reality of the Holy Spirit. We don't know much about them. Perhaps they thought God couldn't be known intimately. However Paul's ministry with them changed their lives. They now experienced the wonder and power of God's presence.

2. a) Why do you think Paul was able to minister to them in this way? See Acts 9:17–20.

   _____

   _____

   _____

   _____

   _____

b) What are some of the things that the Holy Spirit was able to do through Paul himself in Ephesus, according to Acts 19:11–12?

_____

_____

3. Later we will see how some Jews, called the Sons of Sceva, tried to copy Paul. Using the name of Jesus, they also tried to drive out an evil spirit. Read what happened in Acts 19:13–16. How do we know that they were acting in their own power and not in that of the Holy Spirit?

_____

_____

_____

4. You see, it is the Holy Spirit who gives power to Christians to do God's work.

This is a symbol of the Holy Spirit:

The name of Jesus can be used by anybody, whether Christian or not, but only one of these people would be able to do God's work. Think, which one.

a) How, then, do these drawings illustrate the difference between Paul and the sons of Sceva?

b) Even though person "A" says they are a Christian, why is this untrue according to Romans 8:9–10 and John 3:5?

a) _____

_____

b) _____

_____

5. The sons of Sceva realized very quickly that they didn't have the power of Jesus in their lives. When the Christians of Ephesus saw this they became afraid as they realized that fraudulent people would be shown up by the Holy Spirit.

a) Now Jesus said that one of the Holy Spirit's ministries (Jesus called him "the Helper") is to convict us of our sins (John 16:7–8). In what way did the Holy Spirit do this among some of the Christians of Ephesus, and with what results? Read Acts 19:18–19.

_____

_____

b) What lessons should this have for us today?

_____

_____

_____

B. Paul's Teaching on the Holy Spirit in Ephesians

6. Now let's see what Paul teaches about the Holy Spirit in his letter to the Ephesians. We should remember that he wrote this more than 20 years after his conversion. To him the presence and power of the Holy Spirit was not a unique experience in the past, but a lifelong experience of ever **growing** intensity!

    To what **two** things does he liken the Holy Spirit in Ephesians 1:13–14?

    1) _____

    _____

    2) _____

    _____

🖉 **Note:** Underline both of these in your Bible and then write H.S. in the margin by each of them.

7. The same Greek word for "seal" is found in Matthew 27:66. What was "sealed" here, and why?

    _____

8. Look at the picture that illustrates this. Of course, in this case their seal did **not** have the desired effect. Jesus **rose**! However, it does show the importance people attached to seals in those days.

What then do you think Paul meant to teach us by saying the Holy Spirit "seals" us?

_____

_____

9. Now let's look at the second illustration Paul uses for the Holy Spirit: that of a **deposit** which acts as a **guarantee**. Study these pictures.

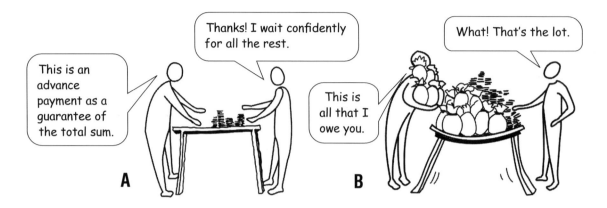

    Which of these pictures is an example of the illustration Paul gives us of the Holy Spirit in Ephesians 1:14 and why?

    _____

    _____

    _____

10. Paul knew the effect of this priceless gift in his own life. He knew, too, that this gift had **power**! Paul uses a wonderful word to describe the **power** of the Holy Spirit. From the word Paul used we get our words "dynamite" (explosive power, mighty strength) and "dynamic" (powerful) and "dynamo" (one of our constant sources of power today). Read Ephesians 1:17–20 and find out what God's **power** (dynamic force) was able to do.

    (Write H.S. in the margin of these verses and underline the two appearances of the word "power")

    a) According to this passage how did God use His **power** in the life of Christ and which of the pictures below illustrates this?

        _____

    b) What will this same power do for us, according to Romans 8:11 and picture B below?

        _____

        _____

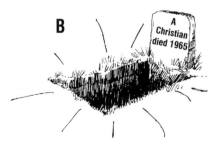

11. So in Ephesians 1:13–20 Paul has given us **three** vivid illustrations of the Holy Spirit. Look again at this short passage and, as review, make sure that you know what these three illustrations are and where you can find them in your Bibles (you should have them marked). Check up with the drawings in the lesson to fix them further in your mind.

    1) _____

    2) _____

    3) _____

12. To Paul the Holy Spirit was not only God's **seal** and his **guarantee** but he also brought Christ's **dynamic power** right into the life of each believer.

    To conclude we must note how Paul sees the power of the Holy Spirit as being much more than just doing miracles or even of raising Christians from the dead on the last day.

    Read Ephesians 3:16. What kind of strength does Paul envisage in the life of a Spirit-filled Christian according to the following references? We'll share the verses around and then pool our results, but make sure that you all write H.S. by each verse, as they are considered:

    Ephesians 3:16–19; 4:3; 5:18–20

    - _____
    - _____
    - _____
    - _____
    - _____
    - _____
    - _____
    - _____

13. What a lovely picture Paul had of a Spirit-filled life! We have seen that his **life** in Ephesus echoed his **teaching** in Ephesians. Let's pray now that our lives may also echo what we have studied together.

14. When you get home, after the Group Meeting, please do

    a) the test for Lesson 1C.

    b) Lessons 2A and 2B which tell us how the Good News spread throughout Asia, and how a great fire for Christ was lighted in Ephesus itself! Then do the tests for these lessons.

    c) Finally do Lesson 2C. Remember to leave the test until after the Group Meeting.

Lesson 2A

The Lecture Hall of Tyrannus, in Ephesus

(Acts 19:8–20)

Do Test 1C before starting this lesson, when we will see how wonderfully the Christian message spread:
 A. Throughout Asia
 B. In Ephesus itself

A. Throughout Asia

1. As was his custom, Paul started his ministry in Ephesus by preaching about the Kingdom of God in the Jewish a) _____ (Acts 19:8); this he did for a period of b) _____ months (Acts 19:8).

2. Then, as in most of the other cities, the unbelieving Jews made things so difficult that Paul withdrew and instead went and held discussions in the a) _____ _____ of b) _____ (Acts 19:9); this he did for a period of c) _____ years (Acts 19:10).

3. Remember that on his **second** missionary journey he had stayed in **Corinth** for a a) _____ and a _____ (Acts 18:11). Now on his **third** missionary journey he taught in the lecture hall of Tyrannus for a period of b) _____ years (Acts 19:10). So he stayed longer in the city of c) _____ than in d) _____ .

4. People used to come from far and wide to Ephesus, and during these two fruitful years many flocked to hear Paul and were converted. The result was that the lecture hall of a) _____ (Acts 19:9) became a center where many people, both b) _____ and _____ (Acts 19:10), heard the word of the Lord, which then spread throughout the whole province of c) _____ (Acts 19:10).

5. As a result, new churches began to spring up in the surrounding towns of the province. You can see three of these marked on the map. They are a) C_____, b) L_____ and c) H_____ , all in the province of d) _____ .

> Hierapolis •
> Laodicea • •
> • Ephesus   Colossae (P)
>
> **ASIA**

Answers

1. a) synagogue
   b) 3
2. a) lecture hall
   b) Tyrannus
   c) 2

3. a) year/ half
   b) 2
   c) Ephesus
   d) Corinth
4. a) Tyrannus
   b) Jews/ Greeks
   c) Asia

5. a) Colossae
   b) Laodicea
   c) Hierapolis
   d) Asia

6. One of those who probably came to Ephesus, and was converted when he met Paul in the lecture hall of Tyrannus, was a wealthy slave owner called a) _____ (see verse 1 and 4 of Philemon). He came from and lived in the neighboring town called b) _____ (marked on the map by the letter "P"). So when this man returned home Paul sent one of his young helpers along with him to evangelize there. This evangelist was c) _____ (Col. 1:7), and as a result of his ministry there was soon a church in Colossae, meeting in the house of d) _____ (Philemon vv.1–2).

7. Now let's see what Paul says about Epaphras in the letter he wrote to the church in Colossae. Read Colossians 4:12–13. Here we see that Epaphras not only established a church in Colossae but also in the two neighboring towns of a) L_____ (Col. 4:13; see map) and b) _____ (Col. 4:13; see map). All these churches were in the province of c) _____ (see map).

8. Although Paul worked hard for these new churches in the ways we have seen, he was never actually able to visit them, and therefore he didn't know most of them _____ (Col. 2:1).

9. Later, Paul was also able to keep in touch with these churches through his ministry of letter writing. For example, we can see from his letter to the church in Colossae that he also wrote a letter to the neighboring church in a) _____ (Col. 4:16) and that he actually expected these two churches to exchange letters! We have one of these two letters in the New Testament; it is the letter to b) _____. Unfortunately the other has been lost, that is the letter to c) _____. He also wrote a **personal** letter to the wealthy slave owner in Colossae, his letter to d) _____.

10. By now you should have a clear picture of how Paul was able to see churches established in the other towns of Asia although he himself never left Ephesus. He did this in three ways:

    1) People from these places were converted when they came to Ephesus and heard **Paul preaching** in the lecture hall of a) _____ (Acts 19:9). They then carried the Good News back to their home towns.

    2) Paul sent out **evangelists** from Ephesus to these towns. One of these was b) _____ (Col. 4:12–13) who visited the towns of c) _____, d) L_____ and e) H_____.

    3) Later, Paul also sent **letters** to these new churches. Two of these we have in the New Testament: his **personal** letter to the converted slave owner f) _____ and his general letter to the church in the same town of g) _____. Another letter has been lost; that is the letter to the h) _____.

Answers

6.	a) Philemon	8.	personally	10.	a) Tyrannus
	b) Colossae	9.	a) Laodicea		b) Epaphras
	c) Epaphras		b) Colossae		c) Colossae
	d) Philemon		c) Laodicea		d) Laodicea
7.	a) Laodicea		d) Philemon		e) Hierapolis
	b) Hierapolis				f) Philemon
	c) Asia				g) Colossae
					h) Laodiceans

11. This picture shows how the Christian message spread throughout Asia.

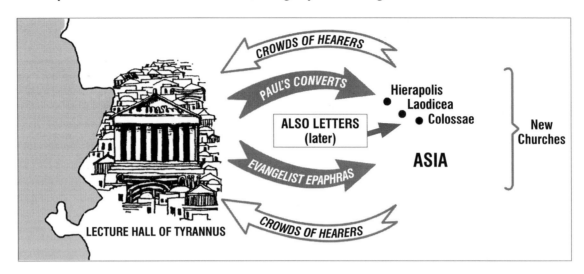

According to the picture,

a) the message spread throughout Asia in three ways. By:

1) _____ _____ 2) _____ 3) _____

b) three daughter churches were established from Ephesus. These were:

1) _____ 2) _____ 3) _____

*We have seen how wonderfully the message spread **throughout Asia**. Now we will see what happened **in Ephesus** itself.*

B. In Ephesus

Read carefully Acts 19:11–20.

12. Look at the three pictures on the next page; they illustrate what took place in Ephesus itself. Of these three pictures, the one that illustrates

a) how the church in Ephesus was purified is Picture _____.

b) how Paul did unusual miracles is Picture _____.

c) how the sons of Sceva failed to do the same is Picture _____.

Answers

11. a) 1) Paul's converts
    2) Evangelists
      (Epaphras)
   3) Letters
  b) 1) Hierapolis
    2) Laodicea
    3) Colossae

12. a) C
  b) A
  c) B

A

(Acts 19:11–12)

B

(Acts 19:13–16)

C

(Acts 19:17–20)

13. Remarkable things were happening in Ephesus itself. God began performing miracles through Paul, like healing people who were a) _____ (Acts 19:12) and turning out of others b) _____ _____ (Acts 19:12).

14. As we can see from Picture A in Frame 12, the most unusual things were used to heal the sick. Two of these things were Paul's a) _____ (sweat bands) and his b) _____ (Acts 19:12).

15. On seeing this, a group of Jews began imitating Paul; they were a) _____ brothers (Acts 19:14), all sons of a Jewish chief priest called b) _____ (Acts 19:14). In the name of Jesus they tried to drive out of a man an c) _____ _____ (Acts 19:13).

16. The man with the evil spirit immediately realized that they were using the name of Jesus without actually knowing the Lord himself. So with terrific violence he attacked and a) _____ (Acts 19:16) them, leaving them b) _____ (Acts 19:16) and with their clothes torn off (see Frame 12, Picture B).

17. This really shook the people in Ephesus. Those who came to believe in Christ openly confessed that they had been practicing a) _____ (Acts 19:18) and bringing out their scrolls they b) _____ these publicly. When they added up the total price of all these books it came to c) _____ (Acts 19:19).

18. So both in the city of a) _____ itself and throughout all the province of b) _____ the word of the Lord kept c) sp_____ and d) g_____ stronger (Acts 19:20).

19. Now one further point. At this time Paul must have written a letter to the church in Corinth warning them of the danger of mixing with _____ _____ (read 1 Cor. 5:9). Like his letter to Laodicea this earlier letter to Corinth, mentioned in what we now call 1 Corinthians, has been lost.

20. In 1 Corinthians 5:10–11, Paul clarifies what he had written in his previous letter, explaining that they should not associate with anyone claiming to be a _____ or _____ but is sexually immoral or greedy, an idolater or slanderer, a drunkard or swindler.

21. Look at Item 2 in Supplement 2. Note how we call letter No.1 the "p_____" letter because it was written before, or previous to, 1 Corinthians. (Write "previous" in the margin by 1 Corinthians 5:9)

22. **To Think and Pray About**

    One of the things that pervades our society today is every kind of manifestation of the occult, from horoscopes to black magic.

Answers

13. a) ill	15. a) seven	18. a) Ephesus
b) evil spirits	b) Sceva	b) Asia
14. a) handkerchiefs	c) evil spirit	c) spreading
b) aprons	16. a) overpowered	d) growing
c) tents	b) bleeding	19. immoral people
	17. a) sorcery	20. brother/ sister
	b) burned	21. "previous"
	c) 50,000 drachmas (silver coins)	

Everything associated with the occult is strictly forbidden by God.

Read carefully: Leviticus 20:6; Deuteronomy 18:9–15; Isaiah 2:6 and 8:19–20.

In the New Testament, one of the marks of real faith was a complete turning away from these things, as happened in Ephesus. Read again Acts 19:18–20.

To be true to Christ we too must do the same because, however trivial these practices may seem to us, they are not to God. It is of course the Holy Spirit who alone can free us from these chains, so earnestly ask his help now.

23. Now review and then do Test 2A

Lesson 2B

Bad News from Corinth

1 Corinthians Written

(Acts 19:21–22)

1. Paul's **third** missionary journey was now well advanced, as he had preached in the synagogue for a) _____ months (Acts 19:8), and had been b) _____ years (Acts 19:10) teaching and discussing in the lecture hall of c) _____ (Acts 19:9). The church in Ephesus and those in the surrounding towns were now strongly established.

2. So Paul began to think of moving on and he decided to visit again the churches he had established on his **second** missionary journey in the provinces of a) _____ and b) _____ (Acts 19:21). After this he planned to take the money he had collected for his Aid programme up to the city of c) _____ (Acts 19:21). Then finally he hoped he would be able to visit the capital of the Empire, that is d) _____ (Acts 19:21).

3. Before visiting Macedonia, Paul sent ahead of him, to prepare the way, (along with one of his new young helpers, Erastus) his beloved "son" in the faith, a) _____ (Acts 19:22), while Paul himself stayed on in Ephesus, to wind up his very successful ministry in the province of b) _____ (Acts 19:22).

    Wherever there is blessing the devil soon counterattacks. Suddenly Paul was attacked in two ways:

    *   Tribulation in Ephesus

    *   Bad news from Corinth

4. Look at the pictures about this on the following page and see how

    a) the tribulation in Ephesus is illustrated by Picture _____.

    b) the bad news from Corinth is illustrated by Picture _____.

Answers		

1. a) three
   b) two
   c) Tyrannus
2. a) Macedonia
   b) Achaia
   c) Jerusalem
   d) Rome
	3. a) Timothy
	   b) Asia
		4. a) A
		   b) B

A. Tribulation in Ephesus (Picture A above)

5.   Suddenly the enemies of the gospel in Asia launched a terrible attack against Paul. We can see this clearly from what he wrote shortly after in 1 and 2 Corinthians. Read for example what he says in 2 Corinthians 1:8–9.

Here we can see that he passed through such trouble while he was in the province of a) _____ (2 Cor. 1:8) that he gave up all hope of staying b) _____ (2 Cor. 1:8). Things were so bad that it was as if Paul and his companions were under a sentence of c) _____ (2 Cor. 1:9). Indeed it was only the Lord himself who d) _____ them from such deadly perils (2 Cor. 1:10).

6. Paul seems to be describing the same troubles in 1 Corinthians. On the one hand he had real opportunities for great and a) _____ work (1 Cor. 16:8–9); but on the other hand he tells of many who were b) _____ him (1 Cor. 16:9). Their opposition became so fierce that it was just as if he had had to fight with c) _____ _____ (1 Cor. 15:32) in the city of d) _____ (1 Cor. 15:32). In Picture A, in Frame 4, Paul imagines a wild beast in the form of a savage e) _____.

✎ **Note:** Some experts think Paul was actually imprisoned in Ephesus and was describing how he was miraculously saved by the Lord from the mouths of the savage wild beasts to which he had been thrown in the Roman arena. However, in this Course, we follow the more traditional view that Paul was merely using picture language here.

7. A careful look at Paul's letter to the Romans (which he wrote shortly after this) seems to reveal further evidence of this terrible ordeal in Asia. Here Paul says that a) _____ and b) _____ had risked their lives for him (Rom. 16:3–4). Of course, this could have happened when they were together in Corinth earlier, but it seems more likely that he is referring to where they lived now, that is, the city of c) _____ (Acts 18:19). But Satan also attacked Paul from another direction.

B. Bad News from Corinth (Picture B)

8. On top of all these troubles in Ephesus Paul suddenly received bad news from the church in Corinth from some members of the family of a) _____ (1 Cor. 1:11). They told Paul about the divisions there that had torn the church apart. There appear to have been four parties in conflict, each claiming to back one of the following names: b) _____, c) _____, d) _____ or e) _____ (1 Cor. 1:12).

9. You may remember that it was Apollos who had been instructed by a) _____ and b) _____ (Acts 18:26–27) in Ephesus, before he went on to the province of c) _____ (Acts 18:27) where he ministered in Corinth. We are not to imagine that Apollos was any more responsible for these divisions than Paul.

Indeed we know from 1 Corinthians itself that Apollos was now back in Ephesus with Paul and that Paul actually trusted him enough to want him to d) _____ (1 Cor. 16:12) Corinth again. It was the parties themselves who were using falsely the names of these leaders to try and justify their wrong actions.

Answers

5.	a) Asia	6.	d) Ephesus	8.	c) Apollos
	b) alive		e) lion		d) Peter
	c) death	7.	a) Priscilla		e) Christ
	d) delivered		b) Aquila	9.	a) Priscilla
6.	a) worthwhile (effective)		c) Ephesus		b) Aquila
	b) opposing	8.	a) Chloe		c) Achaia
	c) wild beasts		b) Paul		d) visit

10. Paul not only had news about Corinth from the family of Chloe, but also received a visit (along with Fortunatus and Achaicus) from a) _____ (1 Cor. 16:17) who was one of the first Christian converts in b) _____ (1 Cor. 16:15) and was now one of those c) l_____ (1 Cor. 16:16) in the church in Corinth. These three had brought with them a letter from the church in Corinth in which they had asked Paul's opinion on various d) _____ (1 Cor. 7:1) that were troubling them.

11. So Paul immediately sent off another letter now known as 1 Corinthians, in which he warns them firmly against having a) _____ (1 Cor. 1:10) in the church. In the letter itself we can see that Paul wrote it while he was still in b) _____ (1 Cor. 16:8).

12. **Exercise**

    Underline the word "Ephesus" in 1 Corinthians 16:8 to remind yourself that Paul wrote this letter while he was in that city.

13. **Review**

    The letter Paul wrote to try and correct the **divisions** that had arisen in Corinth was the letter we call a) _____. He wrote it while he was still in the city of b) _____, as we can see from c) 1 Corinthians _____:_____. Look also at 1 Corinthians 15:32 where he speaks again of being in d) _____.

14. If you look back to Lesson 2A.19 and 20 you will see that the letter we call 1 Corinthians was in fact preceded by a letter usually called the a) _____ letter, which unfortunately has now been b) _____, but to which Paul refers in 1 Corinthians 5:9.

15. Now look at Items 1, 2 and 3 in Supplement 2 on Paul's visits and letters to Corinth and use these to answer the following questions.

    a) On which of his journeys did Paul first visit Corinth and establish the church there? _____

    b) On which of his journeys did he send to Corinth his "previous" letter, and 1 Corinthians? _____

    c) From which town did Paul write both these letters? _____

16. At the end of 1 Corinthians Paul sent greetings to the Christians there from all the churches in the province of a) _____ (1 Cor. 16:19), and especially from his friends b) _____ and c) _____ and the church that met in their house in the city of d) _____ (Acts 18:19). This is further evidence that Paul wrote 1 Corinthians from the city of e) _____.

Answers

10. a) Stephanas
    b) Achaia
    c) laboring
    d) matters
11. a) divisions
    b) Ephesus

13. a) 1 Corinthians
    b) Ephesus
    c) 1 Corinthians 16:8
    d) Ephesus
14. a) "previous"
    b) lost
15. a) second

15. b) third
    c) Ephesus
16. a) Asia
    b) Aquila
    c) Priscilla
    d) Ephesus
    e) Ephesus

17. You will remember how Paul first met Aquila and Priscilla in the city of a) _____ (Acts 18:1–2), so the church there knew them well. Then they had moved with Paul to the city of b) _____ (Acts 18:18–19). So you can see why Paul sent greetings from them when he was actually writing from the city of c) _____, where they lived at that time, to the city where they had lived before, that is, the city of d) _____ (Acts 18:1–2).

18. You will also remember how Paul had just sent off (along with Erastus) his "son" a) _____ (Acts 19:22) to go ahead of him to Macedonia, and then on to the province of b) _____ (Acts 19:21) where of course Corinth was situated. So it is not surprising that he told the Corinthians in this letter that they might soon receive a visit from c) _____ (1 Cor. 16:10). It is good to note again how wonderfully Paul's letters confirm the accuracy of what d) _____ wrote in the Acts.

19. But apart from this major problem of divisions in the church which Paul deals with in **chapter 1** of 1 Corinthians, there were a whole lot of other problems he had to correct as well, so for the rest of this lesson we will take a quick look at what these problems were.

20. **In chapter 5**, for example, he deals with a terrible case of sexual sin that had occurred in the church, when a man had actually been sleeping with his _____ _____ (1 Cor. 5:1).

21. **In chapter 6** he deals with the way some Christians in dispute with other Christians had been taking the matter before _____ (that is to say, heathen) judges (1 Cor. 6:1) instead of letting other believers settle it for them.

22. **In chapter 7** he deals with all the different problems that the Corinthians had written to him about on the subject of m_____ (1 Cor. 7:10).

23. **In chapter 8** he deals with the problem of whether it was right or not for Christians to eat food that had been offered to _____ (1 Cor. 8:1), which was widely sold in the market in Corinth.

24. **In chapter 9** Paul answers those who were criticizing him because he did not receive any a) _____ (1 Cor. 9:18) for preaching the Good News. His enemies said that this meant he wasn't a true b) _____ (1 Cor. 9:2) like the Lord's brothers and Peter. Paul replied that he had a perfect c) _____ (1 Cor. 9:11–12) to receive pay, but that he had refused to do so to avoid putting any d) h_____ (1 Cor. 9:12) in the way of the gospel.

25. **In chapters 10 and 11** he deals with problems arising in their celebrations of the a) _____ _____ (1 Cor. 11:20). For example some of them were actually getting b) _____ (1 Cor. 11:21) in these services. Paul solemnly warns them that if anyone is hungry or thirsty he should eat in his own c) _____ (1 Cor. 11:34) and not use or abuse the church services for this.

Answers

17. a) Corinth	18. c) Timothy	24. a) pay
b) Ephesus	d) Luke	b) apostle
c) Ephesus	20. father's wife (step-mother)	c) right
d) Corinth	21. ungodly	d) hindrance
18. a) Timothy	22. marriage	25. a) Lord's Supper
b) Achaia	23. idols	b) drunk
		c) home

26. **In chapters 12, 13 and 14** Paul deals with the use and abuse of the a) _____ of the _____ (1 Cor. 12:4) and gives wonderful teaching on the greatest thing of all, that is b) _____ (1 Cor. 13:13).

27. **In chapter 15** he deals at length with the truth of the a) _____ (1 Cor. 15:12) which some in Corinth were actually denying. If these people are right, Paul says, then our faith is b) _____ (1 Cor. 15:17) and we are still lost in our c) _____ (1 Cor. 15:17). But, Paul thunders out, they are **not** right, because Christ **has** been d) _____ from the _____ (1 Cor. 15:20). And on this triumphant note of the e) _____, Paul ends dealing with the problems that had arisen in Corinth.

28. **In chapter 16** he invites them to contribute to his a) A_____ for Je_____ fund (1 Cor. 16:1) as the churches in b) _____ (1 Cor. 16:1) had already done. He also explains how he hopes to visit them after having passed through c) _____ (1 Cor. 16:5), which, of course, exactly agrees with what we saw in the Acts, that after Macedonia, he hoped to go through the province of d) _____ (Acts 19:21) on his way to e) _____ (Acts 19:21), to deliver his aid fund.

29. Paul signed off his letter by writing: *"I, Paul, write this greeting in my a) _____ _____"* (1 Cor. 16:21) so that there could be no danger of forgery (compare 2 Thess. 3:17). He sat back contented to have covered such a vast range of problems troubling the Corinthian church, all in this one letter that we call b) _____.

30. **To Think and Pray About**

    Now you have got the background to 1 Corinthians, choose the chapter that you think has teaching on **your** particular problem at the moment and then read it prayerfully to find the solution God has for you.

31. Now review and then do Test 2B.

    Do Lesson C in preparation for the Group Meeting.

Answers

26. a) gifts/ Spirit
    b) love
27. a) resurrection
    b) futile
    c) sins
    d) raised/ dead
    e) resurrection

28. a) Aid/Jerusalem
    b) Galatia
    c) Macedonia
    d) Achaia
    e) Jerusalem

29. a) own hand
    b) 1 Corinthians

Lesson 2C

Problems and Solutions in Colossae

(Colossians and Philemon)

1. **Review**

   Look briefly at this map of the churches Paul saw established in Asia (along with those later mentioned by John in Revelation). Then answer the questions below. The gospel certainly made some impact in Asia, didn't it!

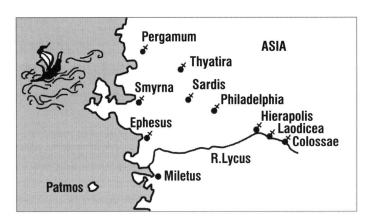

   On the map, which

   a)   was Paul's base while he was in Asia?   _____

   b)   were the three churches he mentions as being ministered to by Epaphras?

   _____   _____   _____

   c)   was the one where he met the elders from
        Ephesus (at the very end of his third journey)?   _____

   d)   was the place where John was later imprisoned?   _____

   e)   were the seven churches to which John wrote in Revelation? (See Rev. 1:11)

   _____

   _____

2. Now let's zoom in on Colossae. Find it in the picture on the top of the next page, nestling in the hills of the Lycus valley. It was relatively small, being overshadowed in importance by the neighboring cities of Laodicea and Hierapolis.

   a)   According to the milestone in the picture on the
        next page, how far inland from Ephesus was Colossae?   _____

   b)   In last week's Group Meeting we studied Ephesians (and its teaching on the Holy Spirit); this week we are going to find out more about the church in Colossae from the two letters Paul wrote to them. Which were these?

   _____

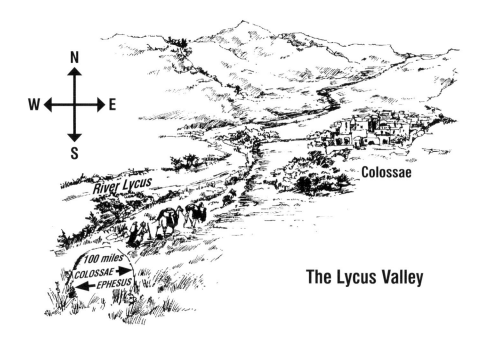

Colossae

The Lycus Valley

A. Epaphras and Philemon: Christian Leaders in Colossae

3. **Review**

   a) Did Paul ever visit Colossae?   _____

   b) Through whom then did they hear the Good News?

   _____

   c) Which other Asian churches did this person help to establish?

   _____

4. Another leading Christian in Colossae was Philemon.

   a) How did Philemon become a Christian? (Philemon, verse 19b)

   _____

   _____

   b) What more can we learn about him from Philemon, verses 1–7 and 15–16.

   _____

   _____

   _____

5. Why do you think Bible students have come to the conclusion that Philemon lived in Colossae, even though this is not mentioned in Philemon? Read Colossians 4:9, 17.

   _____

   _____

B. Problems in Colossae

6. When Paul later wrote to the believers in Colossae it was because someone was disturbing the church with ideas that were not Christian and had nothing to do with the gospel. There were four main problems.

    From each passage given below, make a list of the errors and choose the **two** words you think best sum them up and that could be used as a good **title** for it. (If you use a different version of the Bible, choose the appropriate words.)

    1) Colossians 2:8: _____

        _____

        Title: _____

    2) Colossians 2:16–17, 20b–23: _____

        _____

        Title: _____

    3) Colossians 2:18: _____

        _____

        Title: _____

    4) Colossians 3:5: _____

        _____

        Title: _____

    Discuss the suggested titles and each time you agree on the best title, write this in the "Problems" column in the chart in Test 2C.3, in the box with its reference.

    Each time underline in your Bible the two-word title you have chosen and then write P1, P2, P3, P4 respectively in the margin to remind you of these four Problems.

C. Similar Problems in Our Churches Today

7. What happened in Colossae is happening to us and our churches today! We can say that the "World" (people and ideas not subject to God) tries to weaken our Christian faith and living by adding to or taking away from what Christ has done and revealed. Study this diagram:

Non-Christian ideas

Non-Christian culture and morality

Christian Faith

Christian revelations and teaching

What similar things are attacking our Christian faith and Christ's revelation and teaching in our churches today?

Turn again to the chart in Test 2C.3 and after discussion write in the **"Today's Problems"** column any that we suffer today that are similar to those we have seen in Colossae.

D. Paul's Solutions to these Problems

8. Now let's see what Paul says to counter these ideas! Read one by one his solutions to each of the problems in Colossae. Mark each in your Bible with S1, S2, S3 and S4 respectively.

    | Problem 1 | **Deceptive Philosophy** | Solution 1 | – | Read Colossians 2:2–3, 9–10 |
    | Problem 2 | **Human Commands** | Solution 2 | – | Read Colossians 2:13–15 |
    | Problem 3 | **Unspiritual Mind** | Solution 3 | – | Read Colossians 2:19b and 20a |
    | Problem 4 | **Earthly Nature** | Solution 4 | – | Read Colossians 3:8–10 |

    Review carefully the contents of the chart in the test for Lesson 2C.3 Then, fill out the box entitled **"Solution to our Problem"** with the things that most impressed you from Paul's teaching in Colossians.

9. But the best form of defense is attack! Look at this diagram:

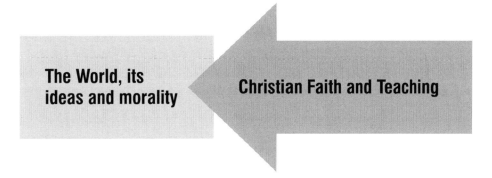

    How can we as Christians "attack" the world's ideas and morality for Christ according to Paul's wonderful teaching in Colossians 3:12–17; 4:2–6?

    _____

    _____

    _____

10. Now let's have a time of prayer based on these things.

11. When you get home, after the Group Meeting, please

    a) do the test for Lesson 2C.

    b) Do Lessons 3A and 3B and their respective tests, in which we will see how in Ephesus Paul's tribulations grew to such an extent that he almost despaired of his life – and how the Lord wonderfully delivered him from everything.

    c) Then do Lesson 3C.

Lesson 3A

Crisis in Corinth: Riots in Ephesus

Paul Leaves for Macedonia (Acts 19:23–41)

A. More Trouble from Corinth

1. Last week we saw how from Ephesus Paul sent 1 Corinthians in an attempt to deal with the problems in Corinth. However, far from seeing an improvement as a result of this letter, Paul soon learned that things were far worse. Indeed, from a careful study of 2 Corinthians it seems certain that things became so bad that Paul actually had to make a quick visit there (a visit not recorded in the Acts) to try and sort things out. This is what is referred to in 2 Corinthians as his a) _____ visit (2 Cor. 13:2) to them. On this visit he must have had a very difficult clash with his opponents. That is why he says in another part that his second visit had been very b) _____ for them (2 Cor. 2:1).

   ✎ **Note:** This quick second visit from Ephesus, not recorded in Acts, is usually called the "painful" visit.

2. Read carefully through Items 1 to 4 in Supplement 2 and use this to answer the following questions.

   a) On which journey did Paul send his first two letters to Corinth (his "previous" letter and 1 Corinthians)? _____ journey.

   b) From which town did he write both of these? _____

   c) From this town Paul made his second visit to Corinth, which we have named his _____ visit.

3. On this "painful" visit Paul must have planned to go to them again in the near future, on his way to a) _____ (2 Cor. 1:16), instead of after visiting b) _____ (1 Cor. 16:5 and Acts 19:21) as he had previously thought. However, due to the unhappy clash with his opponents in Corinth on this "painful" visit, he must have changed his mind again and decided after all **not** to visit c) _____ (2 Cor. 1:23) at that time.

   Because of these changes back and forth in plans, some in Corinth were now saying that Paul was fickle in changing his d) p_____ (2 Cor. 1:17) so frequently. Paul explains to them in 2 Corinthians that he didn't change plans because he was fickle, but in order to e) _____ (2 Cor. 1:23) them any more painful clashes.

Answers

1. a) second
   b) painful

2. a) third
   b) Ephesus
   c) "painful"

3. a) Macedonia
   b) Macedonia
   c) Corinth
   d) plans
   e) spare

---

4. So instead of another painful visit Paul decided to send a severe letter of rebuke. This letter has also been lost, but Paul speaks of it in 2 Corinthians 2:4 where we see that the writing of it caused him great distress and a) _____ of heart and many tears. It appears that this "severe" letter of rebuke really shook the Christians in Corinth, and did what his "painful" visit was not able to do. At any rate we see that through this letter to the Corinthians, Paul caused them b) _____ (2 Cor. 7:8).

5. This letter of sharp rebuke to Corinth is usually called the **"severe"** letter to distinguish it from the earlier one (also lost) which you will remember is called the "previous" letter. (Look back to the note in Lesson 2A.19 and 20). It appears from the way Paul anxiously awaited the return from Corinth of one of his colleagues, with news of how they had received his "severe" letter, that he must have sent this letter by the hand of this old friend from Antioch in Syria, named _____ (2 Cor. 2:13).

6. **Exercise**

    1. Undoubtedly these visits and letters of Paul to Corinth from **Ephesus** form one of the most difficult parts in all Paul's journeys to master. Go carefully through Items 2 to 5 in Supplement 2 to try to get them sorted out in your mind.

    2. Then, go over section A again (Frames 1 to 5 above) before going on to Section B below.

Poor Paul; his opponents in Corinth were causing havoc in the church there and now we will see that things were also going from bad to worse in Ephesus.

B. Worse Trouble in Ephesus

7. Look carefully at the five pictures on the following pages to find out what the new trouble in Ephesus was. They will allow you to answer the questions that follow the last picture.

Answers

4. a) anguish b) sorrow	5. Titus

7. Continued.

D

E

F

Which of the pictures we have just looked at (A, B, C, D, E or F) illustrates each of the following points?

a) The enraged Ephesian mob dragged Gaius and Aristarchus into the theatre.   Picture _____

b) This was because Demetrius, the silversmith had stirred up the mob against Paul.   Picture_____

c) Before Paul arrived, Demetrius did a roaring trade in selling silver temples of the goddess Artemis.   Picture_____

d) But gradually, due to Paul's preaching of Christ, his trade fell away; so he hated Paul.   Picture_____

e) Paul wanted to go to Gaius, but his friends stopped him.   Picture_____

f) When the riot died down Paul left Ephesus, to avoid further trouble.   Picture_____

8.   Read Acts 19:23–27. (Picture A)

One of Paul's principal enemies in Ephesus was a) _____ (Acts 19:24), who was by trade a b) _____ (Acts 19:24), and earned his living, along with many others of his trade, by making silver models of the temple of the goddess, called c) _____ (Acts 19:24), who was worshiped throughout the whole province of d) _____ (Acts 19:27) and throughout the world.

9.   Now read the panel before continuing.

> **PANEL**
>
> **The huge temple of Artemis** stood on the side of a hill overlooking Ephesus; it was so magnificent that it was counted as one of the seven wonders of the world. It was the largest building in the western world. It had 117 slender columns, each 60 feet high and weighing 15 tons. Behind the high altar stood the goddess Artemis, carved out of a black meteorite (see Acts 19:35). The chest of the great idol was covered by breasts to show that Artemis was the goddess of fertility (however the sexual sins here were not as infamous as those associated with Corinth's Aphrodite or Apollo).

One of the seven wonders of the world stood in the great city of Ephesus; this was the temple of the goddess a) _____ (see panel). The goddess herself was a great black idol. Her chest was covered with breasts because she was the goddess of b) _____

Answers

7.		8.		9.	
a)	D	a)	Demetrius	a)	Artemis
b)	C	b)	silversmith	b)	fertility
c)	A	c)	Artemis		
d)	B	d)	Asia		
e)	E				
f)	F				

(see panel). Her worshipers engaged in all kinds of sexual sins, although these were not as outrageous as in the case of the two terrible idols in Corinth, that is the goddess called c) _____ (see panel) and her male counterpart, called d) _____ (see panel).

10. Now the tremendous growth of the gospel, not only in Ephesus, but throughout the whole province of a) _____ (Acts 19:26) had led to a serious drop in the sales of the b) _____ models (Acts 19:24) of the c) _____ of Artemis (Acts 19:24) which were made by d) _____ (Acts 19:24) and his fellow craftsmen (Picture B). So not surprisingly, he was outraged and, calling together the others, he began speaking fiercely against "this fellow" e) _____ (Acts 19:26; Picture C).

11. Now read Acts 19:28–34. The news spread like wildfire throughout the city and soon a great mob was rioting, chanting the slogan over and over again: *"Great is _____ of the _____ !"* (Acts 19:28).

12. The rioting mob seized two of Paul's traveling companions, called a) _____ and b) _____ (Acts 19:29), both from the province of c) _____ , and dragged them into the vast d) _____ (Acts 19:29; Picture D).

✎ **Note 1**:This theatre could accommodate 25,000 people, so just imagine the size of this mob!

✎ **Note 2**:Aristarchus and Gaius were converted on Paul's second missionary journey (Aristarchus in Thessalonica). It's nice to see how many of Paul's converts from his earlier first and second journeys were still helping him on this, his third journey.

13. Immediately Paul learned what had happened to his two friends, a) _____ and b) _____ , he wanted to go before the c) _____ (Acts 19:30), but on seeing the extreme danger of the situation, the other believers d) _____ ____ _____ _____ (Acts 19:30; Picture E).

14. Things were getting more and more out of hand: some were shouting one thing, others were shouting something else. Most of them hadn't a clue what it was all about; it was just mob hysteria. They kept chanting over and over again: *"Great is a) _____ ____ _____ _____ !"* (Acts 19:34) over a period of b) _____ hours! (Acts 19:34)

15. Now read Acts 19:35–41. Eventually the mob calmed down and went home, thanks to the wise intervention of the a) _____ _____ (Acts 19:35). He pointed out to the crowd that Paul had done nothing illegal, and therefore the mob would be in danger of being accused of b) _____ (Acts 19:40) before the Roman officials.

Answers

9. c) Aphrodite
   d) Apollo
10. a) Asia
    b) silver
    c) temple
    d) Demetrius
    e) Paul

11. Artemis/ Ephesians
12. a) Gaius
    b) Aristarchus
    c) Macedonia
    d) theatre
13. a) Gaius
    b) Aristarchus

13. c) crowd
    d) would not let him
14. a) Artemis of the Ephesians
    b) two
15. a) city clerk
    b) rioting

16. Paul saw that his continuing presence in Ephesus was only bringing danger to his Christian friends and so he decided to move on to a) _____ (Acts 20:1; Picture F). As he tells us in 2 Corinthians, he went via b) _____ (2 Cor. 2:12) where he found the way c) o_____ for his preaching (2 Cor. 2:12). Here he anxiously awaited the return of d) _____ (2 Cor. 2:13) with news from Corinth of how they had received his "severe" letter. But he waited in vain and eventually decided to move on to e) _____ (2 Cor. 2:13) and await him there instead. In Macedonia he would have come first to **Philippi**. In our next lesson we will learn what happened.

17. **To Think About**

    The scenes shown in the pictures below must have been occurring simultaneously when Paul was in Troas, but in four **different** places at once.

    a) Check carefully the position on the map of each of these important places. The letter marking the position of Ephesus is a) _____; of Troas is b) _____; of Philippi is c) _____; and of Corinth is d) _____.

    b) Read and think carefully about each of the pictures. According to the pictures, what was happening simultaneously in each of these places at the actual time that Paul was in Troas on this occasion?

18. Now review and then do Test 3A.

Answers

16. a) Macedonia
    b) Troas
    c) opened
    d) Titus
    e) Macedonia

17. a) L
    b) Z
    c) Q
    d) R

Lesson 3B

Macedonia, after Six Years away

(Acts 20:1–2a)

In this lesson we will see two aspects of Paul's **outreach from Macedonia** (probably based in Philippi).
1. Evangelism in Illyricum (Albania and Southern Yugoslavia) (Rom. 15:19, 23a.)
2. Letter to Corinth (2 Corinthians) (2 Cor. 8:16–17)

1. a) Which of the pictures below illustrates Title 1?   Picture _____

    b) And which Title 2?   Picture _____

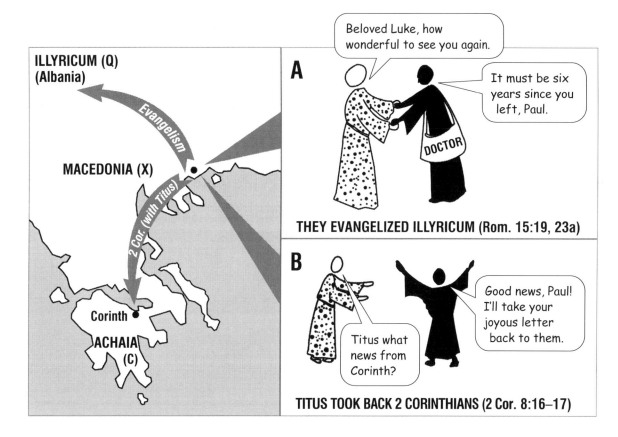

Answers

1. a) A
    b) B

2. After the intense tribulations through which Paul had passed in Asia, it must have been like a breath of fresh air for him to be back in his beloved Macedonia after all those years, marked on the map in Frame 3B.1 by the letter a) _____. Here he met up again with so many dear friends, in the churches he had established in Macedonia on his **second** missionary journey. These you may remember were the churches in b) _____ (Acts 16:12) c) _____ (Acts 17:1) and d) _____ (Acts 17:10).

3. According to our calculations (see note at foot of Supplement 1) Paul had been about 50 years old on that occasion; he was now about 56. So we can calculate that he hadn't seen all these Christian friends for about a) _____ years (calculate from Paul's age). You will remember that Paul spent b) _____ year and a half (Acts 18:11) in Corinth, and c) _____ years (Acts 20:31) in Ephesus. After leaving Corinth and before reaching Ephesus he also made visits to the two important churches of d) _____ and e) _____ (Acts 18:22).

Imagine his joy on meeting up again with the writer of the Acts, who (we discovered from the disappearance of the "we" passages) had stayed on in Philippi; he was the dear doctor f) _____ (Col. 4:14). Probably Paul would also have had fellowship again with g) _____ (Acts 16:14) and the converted h) _____ (Acts 16:33) as well as with their families and the new Christians who had been converted since he left. What a joyous party it must have been!!

4. We are not to think, however, that everything was a bed of roses after leaving Asia. As Paul was soon to report in 2 Corinthians, even in Macedonia he had no a) _____ (2 Cor. 7:5). However, nothing could stop this amazing man of God. With fresh determination he now set off to carry the gospel to all the surrounding areas, actually reaching as far as b) _____ (Rom. 15:19), marked on the map in Frame 1 of this lesson by the letter c) _____. This is our modern d) _____ (see map). There is no doubt that he would have been encouraged and supported in this ministry of outreach by the churches in Macedonia, especially Philippi.

5. It was tough going for a man of 56 but the Lord was more than sufficient.

Read Paul's testimony in 2 Corinthians 4:7–12 where he says:

"We are a) _____ _____ on every side, but not b) _____ (v.8); c) p_____, but not in d) _____ (v.8); e) p_____, but not f) _____ (v.9); g) _____ _____, but not h) _____ (v.9).

6. This was a great period of renewed **expansion** for Paul (see following note). It was also a time of great **consolidation** as we can see from the arrival of a) _____ (2 Cor. 7:6–7) from Corinth, bringing as he did good news on the effect of the "**severe**" letter. So Paul decided to send b) _____ (2 Cor. 8:16–17) back to Corinth, this time with the letter we call **2 Corinthians** in his hand. Corinth was, of course, in the province of c) _____

Answers

2.	a) X	3.	e) Antioch	5.	a) hard pressed	6.	a) Titus
	b) Philippi		f) Luke		b) crushed		b) Titus
	c) Thessalonica		g) Lydia		c) perplexed		c) Achaia
	d) Berea		h) jailer		d) despair		
3.	a) six	4.	a) rest		e) persecuted		
	b) one		b) Illyricum		f) abandoned		
	c) three		c) Q		g) struck down		
	d) Jerusalem		d) Albania		h) destroyed		

(2 Cor. 1:1), marked on the map in Frame 3B.1 by the letter d) _____. Check up that you know where the provinces of Macedonia, Illyricum and Achaia are on the map.

So let's retrace our steps and go over the story of Titus and how he carried these two letters to Corinth for Paul, the "severe" letter from Ephesus, and now 2 Corinthians from Macedonia (probably Philippi).

✎ **Note to Frame 6:** This amazing period of renewed expansion in Macedonia and Illyricum (Rom. 15:19) is only mentioned in passing in Acts 20:1–2a. This is possibly because Luke was too humble to dwell upon a success story that could have been largely supported by his own church in Philippi.

A. Titus Carried "Severe" Letter to Corinth: from Ephesus

(2 Corinthians 2:1–13 and chapter 7)

7. **Review**

    You should remember from our studies in Book 1 that Titus was the young man who over 10 years before had accompanied Paul and Barnabas on their visit from Antioch in Syria to a) _____ (Gal. 2:1), when they had first taken b) _____ (Acts 11:29–30) to the poor there. On this occasion false teachers had wanted to c) _____ him (Gal. 2:3–4), but Paul didn't allow this because Titus was a pure-blooded d) _____ (Gal. 2:3).

8. It seems that Titus had joined Paul's missionary team in Ephesus. As Corinth was largely a Gentile church, Titus, being a Gentile Christian, was especially qualified for the delicate mission of carrying Paul's "severe" letter there. In 2 Corinthians Paul describes how, on leaving Ephesus, he had awaited in vain, in an anguish of worry, for Titus' return; this was in the town of a) _____ (2 Cor. 2:12). Finally he had decided to move on to b) _____ (2 Cor. 2:13) and wait for him there.

9. When eventually Titus did arrive, Paul was already in a) _____ (2 Cor. 7:5). He was immensely b) _____ (2 Cor. 7:6) by Titus' report. In spite of the delicacy of bearing such a "severe" letter of rebuke, Titus had acted at all times with great c) _____ (2 Cor. 7:15) toward the Corinthians. As a result he had won their confidence to such an extent that they were ready to d) _____ all his instructions (2 Cor. 7:15).

10. One of the things Paul had had to rebuke most sharply, both on his "painful" visit to Corinth and in his "severe" letter, was the terrible case of sexual sin mentioned in 1 Corinthians of a man who was actually sleeping with his a) _____ _____ (1 Cor. 5:1). Now at last, they seemed really to feel b) _____ (2 Cor. 7:8) about this terrible sin in the church, and as a result they had c) _____ (2 Cor. 7:9). Whereas before they had actually been d) _____ (1 Cor. 5:2) of this event, as a result of Paul's "severe" letter, they had at last

Answers

6. d) C	8. a) Troas	10. a) father's wife
7. a) Jerusalem	b) Macedonia	b) sorrow
b) help	9. a) Macedonia	c) repented
c) circumcise	b) comforted	d) proud
d) Greek	c) love	
	d) obey	

taken it seriously and had duly e) _____ (2 Cor. 2:6) the offender, which in turn had led to his repentance. Thanks to this, Paul was now able to ask them to f) _____ (2 Cor. 2:7) the man and encourage him to continue in a better way.

B. Titus Carries 2 Corinthians to Corinth: from Macedonia

(2 Corinthians, chapters 8 and 9)

11. So we can see that Titus' mission to Corinth with Paul's "severe" letter had amazing success. It is not surprising, therefore, to find that Paul asked a) _____ (2 Cor. 8:16–17) if he would go back to Corinth ahead of him, carrying with him a new letter, **2 Corinthians**.

    Paul's main reason for sending Titus this time was to make sure that they would be absolutely b) r_____ (2 Cor. 9:3) with their contribution, as part of Paul's programme of aid for Jerusalem in the province of Judea. Notice, Titus was the very man who 10 years previously had accompanied Paul and Barnabas in taking the first Christian aid ever, that was from Antioch in Syria to c) _____ (Acts 11:29). No wonder he was so respected by all the churches.

🖉 **Note 1:** Titus remained one of Paul's faithful helpers to the end. Paul wrote one of his last letters to Titus; when we study it we will see that Titus was looking after the church in Crete at that time.

🖉 **Note 2:** Chapters 8 and 9 of 2 Corinthians are entirely devoted to Titus' mission to Corinth on the matter of the aid program for the poor in Jerusalem.

C. Core Resistance in Corinth

(2 Corinthians, chapters 10, 11, 12 and 13; also 1:12–24)

12. Although Titus had been able to report that almost the entire church was now wanting to show that they had been a) _____ (2 Cor. 7:11) in all these problems, nevertheless there still remained a small pocket of resistance made up of those who were trying to undermine Paul's authority as God's apostle by claiming that he was acting in a b) _____ or selfish manner (2 Cor. 1:17).

13. One of the things that these men were saying about Paul was that he was fickle, in that he kept changing his a) p_____ (2 Cor. 1:17). This was because on his "painful" visit he had said he would visit Corinth on his **way to** b) _____ (2 Cor. 1:16) and then having thought better of it had decided not to go directly to c) _____ (2 Cor. 1:23) but to send his "severe" letter with Titus instead. So in 2 Corinthians Paul defends himself by saying that he was not fickle, because he didn't change his plans for d) _____ motives (2 Cor. 1:17) but only in order to e) _____ (2 Cor. 1:23) them a further painful encounter.

Answers

10. e) punished	12. a) innocent	13. a) plans
f) forgive	b) fickle	b) Macedonia
11. a) Titus		c) Corinth
b) ready		d) worldly
c) Judea		e) spare

14. In the last four chapters of 2 Corinthians (10 to 13) Paul denounces this little group of opponents in Corinth as being false a) _____ (2 Cor. 11:13) and he reminds the Corinthians again of the b) _____ (2 Cor. 13:10) that the Lord had given him to c) _____ up and not to d) _____ down (2 Cor. 13:10).

D. Paul's Third Visit to Corinth Announced

15. Another reason for writing 2 Corinthians was to tell them that he was ready to make his a) _____ visit (2 Cor. 12:14) to them.

    • His **first** visit was when he established the church, with the aid of b) _____ and c) _____ (2 Cor. 1:19) on his d) _____ missionary journey.

    • His **second** visit was what we called his quick "painful" visit (not recorded in the Acts) when he rebuked them sharply and told them that he would e) _____ no one (2 Cor. 13:2). Underline the word "second".

    • His **third** visit was the one he was announcing in 2 Corinthians where he says, *"this will be my* f) _____ (2 Cor. 13:1) *visit to you"*. Underline the word "third". This is the visit to Corinth that we will be studying next week.

E. Paul's Victory in Tribulation
(2 Corinthians 1:1–11; 2:14 to 7:1)

16. Meanwhile in our Group Study we will look at the most beautiful part of 2 Corinthians, and perhaps of all Paul's writings. It is his simple testimony of all that he learned of Christ in the agony of tribulation through which he had passed in his last days in _____ (2 Cor. 1:8).

17. Now look back to the review of Paul's visits and letters to Corinth, in Supplement 2.

    This is one of the most difficult parts of Paul's ministry to get clearly in one's mind, so go carefully through the review trying to sort it all out, and then fill out the short summary below:

    Paul made a) _____ visits to Corinth,

    and wrote b) _____ letters to Corinth.

18. Now review and do Test 3B. Then do Lesson 3C.

Answers

14. a) apostles	15. a) third	16. Asia
b) authority	b) Silas	17. a) three
c) build	c) Timothy	b) four
d) tear	d) second	
	e) spare	
	f) third	

Lesson 3C
Strength in Weakness
2 Corinthians Written

1. Although Titus (when he met Paul again in Macedonia) had been able to report that things were much better in Corinth, there was still a small group of false apostles who were busy undermining Paul's authority there.

   Their idea of a minister of Christ was a man of status, with impressive living standards, and so they looked down on Paul because of all the hardships he had passed through. To them this humiliation and show of weakness lowered the image of a minister and wasn't acceptable to them.

   But the **true** image of a Christian minister (and remember **every** Christian is a minister, or should be) is in fact the exact opposite of what they thought, as Paul is quick to point out. Indeed, Paul actually **boasted** about the very things these false apostles scorned!

   What kind of things did he boast about, in 2 Corinthians 11:30?

   _____

2. Our idea today of what a minister should be seems often more like that held by the false apostles than Paul's teaching!

   a) In 2 Corinthians 12:10 what are the five things that Paul says he was glad to be able to bear as Christ's minister?

   _____

   b) When was Paul at his strongest in the Lord?

   _____

3. You will remember that Paul had just passed through a period of especially terrible tribulation, and no doubt this was on his mind as he wrote.

   At the top of 2 Corinthians in your Bible write this key:

   S in W = Strength in Weakness

   Read 2 Corinthians 1:8–11 and then write **S in W** in the margin.

   a) Where had he suffered all this?

   _____

   b) How bad had this been?

   _____

   c) Why had God allowed all this to happen?

   _____

   _____

d)   What did God do for him on this occasion?

_____

e)   Who did God use in all probability to save Paul on this occasion?

_____

_____

4.   Furthermore, even after Paul arrived in Macedonia, things were still difficult for him.

a)   What did he find everywhere? Read 2 Corinthians 7:5.

_____

🖉   **Note:** A more exact translation is:

"Without were fightings, within were fears." (A.S.V.)

b)   Whom did God use this time to comfort Paul? (2 Cor. 7:6)   _____

c)   How did he comfort him? (2 Cor. 7:7)

_____

_____

5.   Usually a person tries to cover up their weaknesses and defeats in order to make everything look like success. Why then does Paul relate all these things to the Corinthians? It is because he has **one** supreme purpose.

a)   What is this? Read 2 Corinthians 4:7.

_____

b)   What lovely illustration does Paul use here to bring out his meaning?

_____

_____

6.   A similar example to this could be seen in the story of Gideon who, with only 300 unarmed and weak men, defeated a vast and powerful army. Read how, in Judges 7:19–22.

a)   What was hidden in the **clay jar** each man held in his hand (Judg. 7:16)

_____

b)   So what happened in the middle of the night when suddenly every man broke his clay jar?

_____

c)   How does this illustrate what Paul is saying in 2 Corinthians 4:6–7? Write **S in W** in the margin of these verses and underline the words **"common clay pots"** in v.7.

_____

_____

d)   Look at the following pictures. In which picture
do we see this **illustration** from the Old Testament?   Picture _____

e)   And in which picture do we see the **reality**, as it
     occurred several times in Paul's experience?   Picture _____

What light shone forth?

_____

_____

7.   Now read 2 Corinthians 4:8–11 where Paul shows how again and again his "clay pot" was
     broken in order that God's glory could shine through.

     No doubt Paul remembered Jesus' example when he took a piece of bread and **broke** it, and
     said *"This is my body, which is for you"*. (1 Cor. 11:24)

     Why did Paul glory in the fact that his mortal body was frequently at death's door, just as Jesus
     had been when he lived on earth?

     _____

     _____

8.   The **Group Leader** will read out the following Bible passages, without comment:

     (In each, all should write **S in W** in the margins)

     1 Corinthians 1:23–30; 2 Corinthians 12:7–10; Matthew 16:24–25

9.   Another striking illustration of this tremendous truth is where Paul uses the example of a
     prisoner in the triumphal procession of a returning victorious Roman emperor or general to
     show how a Christian's power is strongest in their weakness.

     First came the conquering hero in his chariot, followed by his troops and prisoners, captive
     kings and princes displayed as trophies of his victory, while fragrant clouds of incense were
     being offered up on every side.

     Read how Paul uses this idea in 2 Corinthians 2:14–16 (by turning all the values upside down)
     and compare it with the following picture. Write **S in W**, in the margin and underline the
     words "Christ's victory procession" in v.14.

In this picture:

a) Who is the victor in the chariot? _____

b) What are the chains that bind his prisoners to his chariot? Look carefully at the picture. _____

c) What is Paul offering up in the procession? _____

d) What are the two reactions to this incense shown by the bystanders?

_____

10. So Christ's captives become victors as well as captives. Their very captivity and weakness is their first taste of perfect freedom and deliverance as they share in the triumph parade of their new Master. Read 2 Corinthians 3:5.

a) From whom does a minister's real strength come?

_____

b) Why can we never claim to be capable in ourselves for this ministry?

_____

11. This then was Paul's idea of a true minister of Christ. He sums it up beautifully in 2 Corinthians 4:5.

✎ **Note:** The word Paul uses here for "servants" really means "slaves".

a) What should a minister **not** preach about?

_____

b) What relationship should ministers have to their people?

_____

c) What should he preach about?

_____

12. Finally, Paul shows that this idea of "strength in **weakness**" is essentially **practical**. Take for example the comforting of a person in deep trouble.

    Read 2 Corinthians 1:4. Write **S in W** in the margin.

    a) Who is the most likely to be able to do this effectively, someone who is always strong and on top of every situation, or someone who has agonized in similar troubles?

    _____

    _____

    b) Why is this?

    _____

    _____

13. Or again, we can see this same truth of strength in weakness shown when a child of God has to face extreme physical weakness and even approaching death, and triumph over it. How can this be, according to Paul in 2 Corinthians 4:16–18? Write **S in W** in the margin.

    _____

    _____

14. To Paul then, the marks of an authentic Christian ministry are to see God's power channeled through humble and weak instruments, so that the glory can be seen to be **his**.

    Does this bring you comfort?

    Read 1 Corinthians 1:26–31 and then 2 Corinthians 4:7, without comment and then we'll have a time of prayer.

15. When you get home please do

    a) the test for Lesson 3C.

    b) Lessons 4A and 4B which tell how Paul moved off from Macedonia and arrived in Corinth, where he wrote his amazing letter to Rome. Then do Test 4A and 4B.

    c) Then do Lesson 4C.

Lesson 4A

Back in Corinth

(Acts 20:2b–3)

Romans Written (Rom. 15:12 to 16:27)

1. Having finished evangelizing in the provinces of a) M______________ and b) I______________ (see the following map) Paul now journeyed south to the province of c) ____________ (Acts 20:2) where he stayed for a period of d) _____ months (Acts 20:3) in the city of e) ______________ (map). This was his f) __________ visit (2 Cor. 12:14) to this city, and, as we have already seen, one of his main objectives was to receive the g) ________ (Rom. 15:26 compare with 2 Cor. 9:5) they had promised to make toward Paul's fund for the h) ________ among God's people in i) ________________ (Rom. 15:26). This he intended to take personally (accompanying the delegates from the donating churches) to j) ________________ (Rom. 15:25).

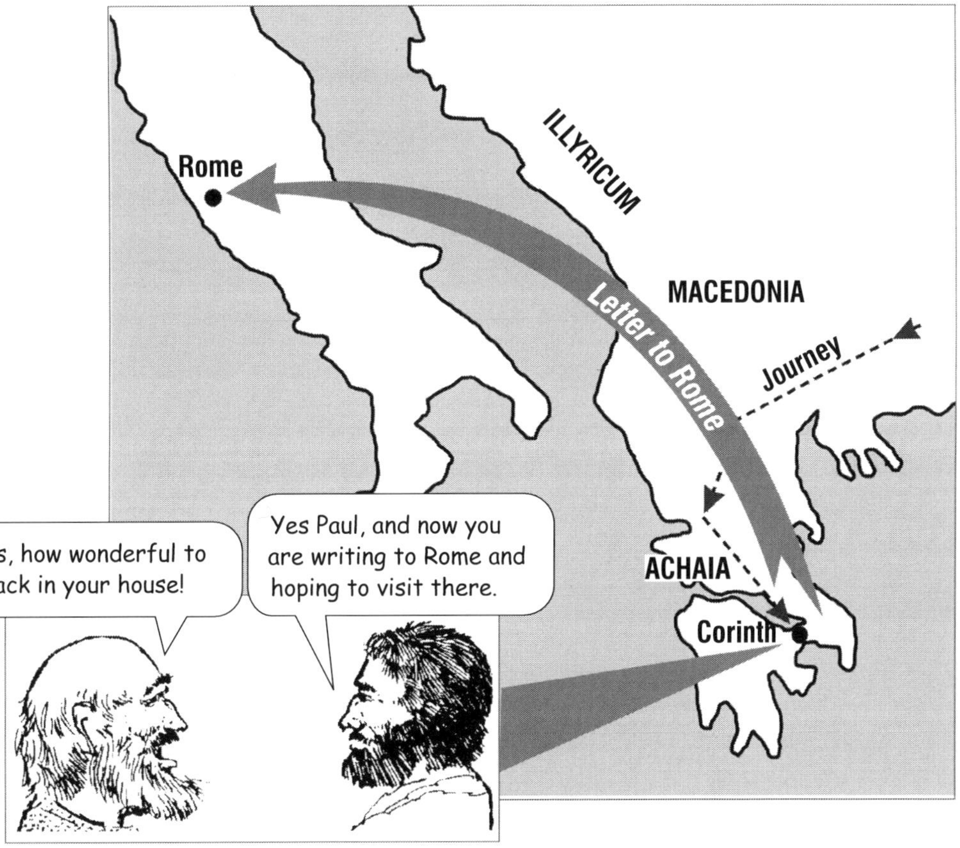

Rome
ILLYRICUM
MACEDONIA
Letter to Rome
Journey
ACHAIA
Corinth
Gaius, how wonderful to be back in your house!
Yes Paul, and now you are writing to Rome and hoping to visit there.

Answers

1. a) Macedonia
   b) Illyricum
   c) Achaia (Greece)
   d) 3
   e) Corinth

1. f) third
   g) gift or offering or aid
   h) poor
   i) Jerusalem
   j) Jerusalem

2. So now we arrive at a truly momentous time in Paul's ministry when, in all sincerity, this mighty man of God could sit back a moment and say with intense satisfaction that he had a) _____ _____ work to do in those regions (Rom. 15:23). By this he meant that he had adequately evangelized all the way from b) _____ to c) _____ (Rom. 15:19). What a gigantic accomplishment!

3. But don't think that this meant that Paul was intending to retire! Although he was now about 57 years old, a vast **new** plan of expansion was forming in his mind, reaching out to the extreme **west**, to the country of _____ (Rom. 15:24).

4. Now take a look at the map to see just how incredible this plan was!

🖉 **Note:** This is not a detailed map of the journeys.

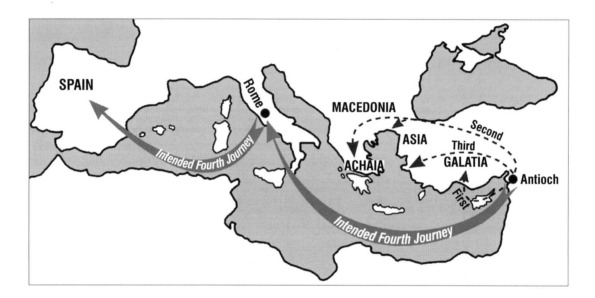

By looking at the distance Paul now **planned** to travel from Antioch in Syria to **Spain**, we can see at a glance that, compared to any of his previous three missionary journeys it is (check the right answer):

☐ a. half the distance.

☐ b. the same distance.

☐ c. more than double the distance.

5. So Paul realized that, just as Antioch in Syria had provided a wonderful **base** from which to launch his first three journeys, he would require a **new** base if he were ever going to evangelize adequately **Spain** and the extreme west.

Answers

2. a) no more
   b) Jerusalem
   c) Illyricum
	3. Spain
	4. c.	

This new base would have to be

- a strong, well established church.

- situated far nearer to **Spain** than was Antioch in Syria.

- suitable for Paul to use for periods of rest.

- willing to help send him out on his new task.

The obvious choice was the church in a) _____ (Rom. 1:7) to which he writes, asking them to b) _____ him (Rom. 15:24) in his new mission to c) _____ (Rom. 15:24) after he had enjoyed visiting them first.

6. The church in Rome was not only suitable as his new base because it was so much nearer to Spain, but also because it contained a large number of Paul's friends and converts who had gravitated there, as it was the capital of the Empire. We know this because in Romans 16 Paul greets them by name. For example he greets his old friends who had returned to Rome from Ephesus, that is a) _____ and b) _____ (Rom. 16:3). Indeed he greets no less than 24 people by name in Romans, chapter c) _____, as well as naming two whole families that he knows!

7. So although Paul had never visited Rome, he obviously looked upon the church there as very close to him. The letter he wrote them is considered by many to be his finest, and indeed it ranks among the greatest writings of all time.

Now review again the three letters (preserved in the New Testament) that Paul wrote on his third missionary journey (in Supplement 1), seeing how Romans is the last of these. From Supplement 1 you can see that Paul was about a) _____ years old when he wrote Romans when he was in the city of b) _____.

8. He was staying in the house of his host, a) _____ (Rom. 16:23) at the time (look again at the picture in 4A.1). It was lovely to be in the home of one of his first converts in Corinth, that Paul himself had b) _____ (1 Cor. 1:14) on his **second** missionary journey, in the very early days in Corinth when he was alone there awaiting c) _____ and d) _____ (Acts 18:5) to follow him on from Macedonia.

9. Furthermore, thanks to Titus' recent successful peace mission to Corinth, Paul was at last able to relax, after the fearful storms through which he and the Corinthian church had just passed. So as a result, in his letter to the Romans, Paul was able to set out his most profound and mature teaching on the a) _____ of Christ (Rom. 1:16); indeed he testifies that he has complete confidence in it because it is God's b) _____ to save all who c) _____, first the d) _____ and also the e) _____ (Rom. 1:16).

Answers

5. a) Rome
   b) assist
   c) Spain
6. a) Priscilla
   b) Aquila
   c) 16

7. a) 57
   b) Corinth
8. a) Gaius
   b) baptized
   c) Silas
   d) Timothy

9. a) gospel
   b) power
   c) believe
   d) Jews
   e) Gentiles

10. His letter to Rome is a most brilliant explanation of how a sinner, whether Jew or Gentile, can be put right with God: it is through a) _____ (Rom. 1:17) from beginning to end. Paul takes Habakkuk 2:4 as his text, then writes: *"The* b) _____ (person who is put right with God) *will* c) _____ *by* d) _____" (Rom. 1:17). This then is **the central theme** of his letter to the Romans.

11. Now it is important both to compare and to contrast Romans with Galatians, because one of the main themes of Galatians is that a person is justified, that is to say a) _____ _____ with God only by b) _____ in c) _____ _____ (Gal. 2:16). So the **theme** of Paul's letter to the Romans is very similar to his letter to the d) G_____.

12. But here the likeness ends! In **style** they are totally different! **One** is like a white hot volcano, erupting in burning indignation against the false teachers who had done such damage to his newly planted churches; this, you will remember, is his letter to the a) _____. The **other** is serene and mellow as he sets out, with brilliant logic, his mature and reasoned reflections on these same truths. This, we have just seen, is his letter to the b) _____.

13. As we study Paul's letter to the Romans we shall see how his purpose is to explain to **two** groups in the church how a sinner can be put right with God by **faith**. These two groups are the a) _____ and the b) _____ (Rom. 1:16). The reason for this is that the church in Rome had a large number of Christians from **both** these groups.

14. Of course, being the capital of the Empire, Rome itself was not a Jewish but a a) _____ city, so the strongest group in the church would probably have been b) _____.

15. On the other hand we know that in Paul's day there was a large colony of Jews in Rome. For example, Philo, a writer of those times, tells us that the Roman Emperor, in power at the time Jesus was born and who was called _____ (Luke 2:1), allowed all the Jews in Rome to practice their religion freely, and gave them a special area, beyond the river Tiber in Rome, where they could meet.

16. To illustrate this, let's go over the movements of the Jewish couple, Aquila and Priscilla, by studying the following three maps.

Answers

10. a) faith	11. a) put right	13. a) Jews
b) righteous	b) faith	b) Gentiles
c) live	c) Jesus Christ	14. a) Gentile
d) faith	d) Galatians	b) Gentiles
	12. a) Galatians	15. Augustus
	b) Romans	

Movements of Aquila and Priscilla

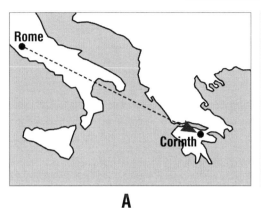

A

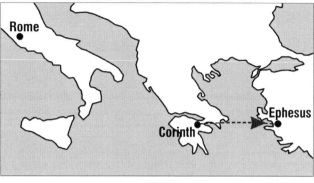

B

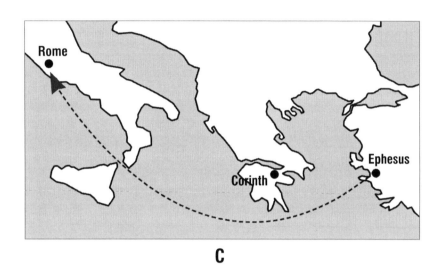

C

When we first heard about them they had been turned out of the city of a) _____ (Acts 18:2) by the Roman Emperor b) _____ (Acts 18:2) because they were c) _____ (Acts 18:2). From there they had gone to d) _____ (Acts 18:1–2) where Paul first met them, as in map e) _____. After that they moved with Paul to f) _____ (Acts 18:19) as in map g) _____. Now Paul's greetings to them in this letter show that they were back safe and sound again in h) _____, as in map i) _____ (where there had been a change of Emperors).

17. Some time before Priscilla and Aquila moved back to Rome, when Paul had still been with them in Ephesus, he also had begun to think of going on from Macedonia, Achaia and Jerusalem to a) _____ (Acts 19:21). Indeed, it could well have been the fact that Priscilla and Aquila were planning to go back to b) _____ that set Paul thinking of following them there!

Answers

16. a) Rome
    b) Claudius
    c) Jews
    d) Corinth

16. e) A
    f) Ephesus
    g) B
    h) Rome
    i) C

17. a) Rome
    b) Rome

18. Well, throughout this study, perhaps you have noticed how much background material we have been able to gather about this letter to the Romans mainly from **three** of its chapters; that is:

- chapter 1 (esp. vv.16–17)

- chapter 15 (esp. v.24)

- chapter 16 (v.3 onwards)

Exercise

Underline in your Bible Romans 1:16–17; Romans 15:24; Romans 16:3.

19. In which of the three chapters, mentioned in Frame 18, does Paul

   a) tell them that the message he wants to share
   with them is how a sinner can be put right with God by faith.   Chapter _____

   b) share his plan to evangelize Spain, and his hope
   that the church in Rome will help him in this
   mission by providing him with a new base.   Chapter _____

   c) greet lots of old friends and converts who had
   gravitated to Rome, which shows us what strong
   links he had with this church.   Chapter _____

20. So in Corinth, during this period of a) _____ months (Acts 20:3), Paul completed this wonderful letter we call Romans. Perhaps another reason for writing it was that a lady called b) _____ (Rom. 16:1), from Corinth's neighboring church, c) _____ (Rom. 16:1), was actually going to travel to Rome, and so Paul was able to take advantage of this by sending his letter with her. He also takes the opportunity of asking the church in Rome to d) _____ her in the Lord's name (Rom. 16:2) and give her all the help she needs.

   This then, in brief, is the story of how, why and what Paul wrote to the Romans.

21. **To Think and Pray About**

   How does Paul try to persuade the Christian **Jews** in Rome to help his mission to the **Gentiles** in Spain? (Read Romans 15:8–12; and 20–21.)

   What great principle does Paul establish here?

   What are you and your church doing to put this principle into practice in your area? What more could you do?

22. Now review and then do Test 4A.

Answers

19. a) 1	20. a) 3
b) 15	b) Phoebe
c) 16	c) Cenchreae
	d) receive

Lesson 4B

Righteousness Needed, Imputed and Imparted

(Romans, Chapters 1 to 8)

This lesson is longer than usual because it covers one of the richest parts of the Bible. Give yourself plenty of time to read these chapters in Romans and to master them and you will never regret it!

Romans, chapters 1 to 8 can be divided as follows:

A. Righteousness **needed** — chapters 1 to 3

B. Righteousness **imputed** — chapters 4 and 5

C. Righteousness **imparted** — chapters 6 to 8

A. Righteousness NEEDED (Chapters 1 to 3)

1. As we have seen, Paul wrote his letter to Rome from the house of Gaius in **Corinth**. Book 2 described how the worship of idols (especially Apollo and Aphrodite) abounded in Corinth. (See Book 2, Lesson 7B.3 and 18 – especially the pictures.)

2. As Paul looked around him in Corinth he was simply appalled by the sin of this vice-ridden city. His reaction to this is clearly reflected in the first 3 chapters of Romans.

    Paul points out that two things that God has **revealed** to us.

    In Romans 1:17 he says that in the a) _____ it is **revealed** how God makes people righteous (puts them right with himself) through faith.

    In Romans 1:18 he says that, on the other hand, God's b) _____ is also **revealed** against all the c) w_____ of people whose evil ways prevent the truth from being known.

Answers

2. a) gospel
    b) wrath
    c) wickedness

---

3. So Paul launches into one of the most penetrating exposures of the sin of humankind that has ever been written, undoubtedly describing what was going on all around him in Corinth. Here are the principal areas of sin that he exposes (but not in the right order):

   • Unnatural sexual acts   • Violence   • Idolatry

   Read carefully the following passages and after each write the **main** sin exposed (choosing from the list above).

   a) Romans 1:18–25   _____

   b) Romans 1:26–27   _____

   c) Romans 1:28–31   _____

   Remember, these were the sins that abounded in this corrupt city where Paul was writing his letter to the Romans, that is, d) _____.

4. Throughout **chapter 1** Paul has been describing the sins of the **Gentiles** in Corinth who were sunk in idolatry (Rom. 1:23). No doubt his Jewish readers would be thinking, "We are not sinners like that; we worship the one true God, so we are all right". So in chapter 2 Paul directs his message to the a) _____ (Rom. 2:17) who relied on the b) _____ and boasted about their relationship with c) _____.

5. Although, in the opening verses of Romans 2, Paul doesn't mention Jews specifically, nevertheless it is clear that he is talking about them **indirectly** even from the **first** verse, when he says, *"You who pass* a) _____ *on someone else"* (Rom. 2:1). Paul then points out that having b) _____ others, they then go on to do the c) _____ things (Rom. 2:1) which the Gentiles do, although of course in a refined way and under the cloak of obeying the Law of Moses. Soon Paul declares openly that, in chapter 2, he is speaking to those who call themselves d) _____, and who depend on the e) _____ (Rom. 2:17).

6. But although the Jews made a pretense at obeying the law, in actual fact they were a) _____ the law (Rom. 2:25b) and so their b) _____ was of no value (Rom. 2:25).

7. Finally, in **Romans 3** Paul draws these **two** lines of argument together when he says: *"We have already made the charge that* a) _____ *and* b) _____ *alike are all under the power of sin"* (Rom. 3:9). Yes, c) _____ (Rom. 3:23), both Jew and Gentile alike, have d) _____ and, as the Good News Bible puts it, are *"far away from God's saving presence"*.

8. I hope you can now see how, in order to show that a person's own righteousness, whether they be Gentile or Jew, is quite insufficient to save them, Paul has proved in chapters 1, 2 and 3 (up to verse 20) that **everyone** has sinned and therefore **needs** the righteousness which Christ

Answers

3.	a) Idolatry	5.	a) judgment	7.	a) Jews		
	b) Unnatural sexual acts		b) judged		b) Gentiles		
	c) Violence		c) same		c) all		
	d) Corinth		d) Jews		d) sinned		
4.	a) Jews		e) law				
	b) law	6.	a) breaking				
	c) God		b) circumcision				

alone can provide for those who have a) _____ in him (Rom. 3:22). Now let's sum up. The main chapter in Romans where Paul deals with the sins of

b)   the **Gentiles** is chapter _____.

c)   the **Jews** is chapter _____.

d)   both **Jew and Gentile** is chapter _____ (up to v.20).

9.   So we have seen that the three chapters in Romans where Paul describes humanity's desperate lack of, and need for, righteousness, are a) _____, _____ and _____ (up to v.20). In this last verse, **Romans 3:20**, Paul concludes by saying that **no one** is put right in God's sight by doing what the b) _____ requires, because this only makes us conscious that we have c) _____. So in these first three chapters Paul has set the stage for answering the basic question of humanity, asked by Job so many years before: *"How then can a mortal be* d) _____ *before God?"* (Job 25:4).

B.   Righteousness IMPUTED (Chapters 4 and 5)

10. In Romans, **chapter 3** (from verse 21) to **chapter 5** the answer comes with dazzling clarity: **God's** way of putting people a) _____ with himself has been revealed (Rom. 3:21). It is apart from the b) _____ (Rom. 3:21); it is through c) _____ in d) _____ _____ alone (Rom. 3:22). We don't have to work for it; it is given to us e) f_____ (Rom. 3:24). This is because Christ died as a f) _____ (Rom. 3:25) so that our sins might be forgiven. Only in this way could God show that he himself is just and righteous (having received the punishment for our sins himself, in Christ on the cross), and yet at the same time can put every sinner who believes in Jesus right with himself without punishing the sinner.

11. **In chapters 4 and 5** Paul gives us the example of **two** Old Testament people to explain this most glorious truth in the minutest detail. The first example is a) _____ (Rom. 4:3) about whom the Old Testament scripture says that because he b) _____, God c) _____ it to him as righteousness, i.e. accepted him as righteous (Rom. 4:3b). This is what is called God's **imputed** righteousness, which means that God clothes believing sinners in Christ's righteousness and then accepts them as if they were his own, as if the believing sinners themselves were righteous.

12. The whole of **chapter 4** is taken up with the beautiful example of the faith of Abraham and how in this way he was accepted as a) _____ by God (Rom. 4:22). And then Paul is quick to point out that the **imputed** righteousness was not for Abraham alone, but also for b) _____ if we have faith (Rom. 4:24). Read the last verse, Romans 4:25, and meditate on its truth.

Answers

8. a) believed	10. a) right	11. a) Abraham
b) 1 c) 2 d) 3	b) law	b) believed
9. a) 1, 2 and 3	c) faith	c) credited
b) law	d) Jesus Christ	12. a) righteous
c) sinned	e) freely	b) us
d) righteous	f) sacrifice	

13. **Romans 4** gives us an example of **likeness**, that of a) _____ (Rom. 4:1). Everything he received through faith, we can also receive (Rom. 4:22–24).

    Romans 5 gives us an example of **contrast**, that of b) _____ (Rom. 5:14). Everything he **didn't** do, Christ **did** do to perfection (Rom. 5:15).

14. Adam was a pattern (or example) of the one who was to come, Christ – but far from being an example of likeness, he was an example of contrast, because the two are not a) _____ one another (Rom. 5:15).

    Here Paul argues that as the **one** sin (of Adam) brought b) _____ to all people (Rom. 5:18), in the same way, by contrast, the **one** righteous act (of Christ) brings c) _____ and d) _____ to all people (Rom. 5:18).

15. Paul's argument here is based upon the **solidarity** of the human race, which, as it caused the downfall of humanity through the first Adam, can in the same way lead to the salvation of humanity by the second Adam, Christ.

    Let's consider this argument. Unlike angels, that neither marry nor have children (Matt. 22:30) all human beings are born of parents from whom they receive their genes, hereditary traits and, unfortunately, their sinful natures.

    So the whole human race fell **together** with its first parent, Adam. Angels, on the other hand, are totally independent beings, each one having been created apart, so they stand or fall **by themselves**. Look at the pictures below.

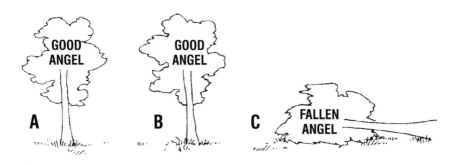

    Angels are like many individual trees, that stand or fall by themselves. One can fall, Tree a) _____, without affecting the others.

Answers

13. a) Abraham
    b) Adam
14. a) like
    b) condemnation
    c) justification
    d) life

15. a) C

But **all human beings** are closely related by birth: the human race is like the many branches of a **single tree** — with its trunk — **Adam**!

When Adam fell, the whole human race, through heredity, fell with him! Tree b) _____ .

But the very factor of the **solidarity** of the human race, which in Adam caused the downfall of all people (Rom. 5:12), leads in the same way to the **lifting up** of all who are united by faith to Christ, the **second** Adam, Tree c) _____ .

16. Read Romans 5:18–19 comparing this with what the pictures illustrate.

    Romans 5:18 teaches that, as the one sin (of Adam) condemned a) _____ people because of the hereditary solidarity of the whole human race, so through the same solidarity of faith, the one righteous act (of the **second** Adam, that is Christ) gives life to b) _____ people who believe in Jesus Christ as Savior.

    Romans 5:19 teaches that just as all people were made c) _____ as a result of the **disobedience** of one man (Adam), in the same way, when they are united to him (Christ) by faith, they will be made d) _____ before God as a result of the **obedience** of the one man (the **second** Adam, that is Christ).

17. Let's summarize the first 5 chapters of Romans:

    We have seen that most of **chapters 1, 2 and 3** were taken up by Paul's exposure of the sin of all people, both Gentile and Jew, and therefore of humanity's lack of righteousness; righteousness **needed**.

    In **chapters 4 and 5** Paul shows how **all** those who put their faith in Christ are accepted as righteous; righteousness **imputed**. He uses two examples of this.

    Who is the person he uses as an example:

    a) by **likeness**, in chapter 4?   _____

    b) by **contrast**, in chapter 5?   _____

Answers

15. b) D
    c) E
16. a) all
    b) all
    c) sinners
    d) righteous

17. a) Abraham
    b) Adam

C. Righteousness IMPARTED (Chapters 6 to 8)

18. But isn't this truth of **imputed** righteousness rather dangerous? If righteousness is indeed a **free gift**, and received by faith alone, without having to do anything to earn it, as Paul said in Romans 4:4–5, couldn't this lead to even more sinful conduct?

    Paul voices this objection in Romans 6:1.

    > "*Shall we* a) _____ _____ *sinning so that grace may increase?*"

    Paul's reaction is clear. He says, b) "_____ _____ _____!" (Rom. 6:2). This would be to miss the whole meaning of faith as a total trusting, commitment to, and union with the risen Lord Jesus who transforms the believer's life.

19. In gratitude and joy for being freely **accepted** as righteous by **faith** in Christ (**imputed** righteousness) the believer begins a new life that is actually **being made** righteous by **union** with Christ (**imparted** righteousness).

    In **Romans 4 and 5** Paul explains the wonderful truth of a) **im**_____ righteousness.

    In **Romans 6, 7 and 8** he develops this exciting new theme of b) **im**_____ righteousness.

20. In Romans 6, 7 and 8 Paul uses three examples, well known in Corinth and to the people of that time, in order to explain **imparted** righteousness:

    1. Baptism – (Romans 6:1–14)

    2. The slave market – (Romans 6:15–23)

    3. Marriage – (Romans 7)

    ### 1. BAPTISM (Romans 6:1–14)

21. **Baptism** is a symbol of a Christian's death and resurrection in union with a) _____ (Rom. 6:3–4). For since we have been united with him in his b) _____ (Rom. 6:5), in the same way we shall be united with him by being c) r_____ to life as he was (Rom. 6:5). So by sharing in his death the power of our old sinful self was d) _____ _____ with (Rom. 6:6). By sharing in his resurrection we now live a e) _____ life (Rom. 6:4) to f) _____ (Rom. 6:10) and in fellowship with him through Christ. This means that we surrender our whole being to him to be used as instruments of g) _____ (Rom. 6:13b). This is **imparted** righteousness.

    ### 2. THE SLAVE MARKET (Romans 6:15–23)

22. In Romans 6:15 Paul repeats his question of Romans 6:1 "*Shall we sin because we are... under grace? By no means!*".

Answers

18. a) go on	21. a) Christ	21. e) new
b) By no means	b) death	f) God
19. a) imputed	c) raised/ resurrected	g) righteousness
b) imparted	d) done away	

To both Jesus and Paul conversion is a change of masters, just as a slave bought in a **slave market** stops obeying his old master and starts obeying his new one.

Jesus said, *"No one can a) _____ two masters!"* (Matt. 6:24). Paul says *"Just as you used to offer yourselves as b) _____* (Rom. 6:19) *to c) _____ and to ever-increasing d) _____, so now offer yourselves as e) _____ to f) _____ leading to holiness."* For a converted **Corinthian** this was really something! This is **imparted** righteousness.

3.   MARRIAGE (Romans 7)

23. In Romans 6:14 Paul says quite clearly to all Christians, *"Sin shall **no longer** be your a) _____, because you are not under the b) _____, but under c) _____."*

    But this raised a big problem for the **Jewish** Christians who had been brought up so strictly under the law. It was just as if they, who had been **married** to the law, were now being married to Christ as well! Didn't this all add up to spiritual marital unfaithfulness?

24. In **Romans 7** Paul speaks to the Jews (see Rom. 7:1) in order to answer this difficulty.

    The marriage bond, he points out, only rules over a couple as long as **both** partners are alive. The moment **either** of them die, the bond is broken.

    Paul gives an **example** from daily life.

    If a woman goes to live with another man while her husband is still alive she would be an a) _____ (Rom. 7:3). If, however, her husband dies, this breaks the marriage bond and she is free to marry another without committing b) _____ (Rom. 7:3). Now in the case of the Christian Jews, they are now released from the c) _____ (Rom. 7:6) which once bound them, because they themselves have d) _____ (Rom. 7:6) to the law. They no longer need to serve in the old way of a written e) _____ (Rom. 7:6), but in the new way of the f) _____ (Rom. 7:6), without falling into spiritual adultery.

25. So remember the examples used in Romans 6 and 7 to make clear his teaching on **imparted** righteousness. They are:

    In chapter 6 a) B_____ and the b) S_____ M_____.

    In chapter 7 c) M_____.

26. **Romans 8** brings this section to a magnificent conclusion by showing how this **imparted** righteousness is possible through being a) _____ Christ (Rom. 8:1) and the presence of the b) _____ of _____ (Rom. 8:9) living in you.

Answers

22. a) serve
    b) slaves
    c) impurity
    d) wickedness
    e) slaves
    f) righteousness
23. a) master

23. b) law
    c) grace
24. a) adulteress
    b) adultery
    c) law
    d) died
    e) law/ code

24. f) Spirit
25. a) Baptism
    b) Slave Market
    c) Marriage
26. a) in
    b) Spirit of God

27. Try and get this simple analysis fixed in your memory by going over the following points and filling them in below. Look back if you are in doubt.

    A.   Righteousness N_____   chapters _____, _____ and _____

    B.   Righteousness Im_____   chapters _____ and _____

        1)   Ab_____ chapter _____

        2)   Ad_____ chapter _____

    C.   Righteousness Im_____   chapters _____, _____ and _____

        1)   B_____, chapter 6

        2)   The S_____ M_____, chapter 6

        3)   M_____, chapter 7

28. **To Think and Pray About**

Read through slowly and thoughtfully Romans 8 at a sitting. Many would call this chapter the climax of the whole Bible message!

29. Now review and then do Test 4B.

Answers

27. A. Righteousness
      Needed/ ch. 1, 2, 3
   B. Righteousness
      Imputed/ ch. 4 and 5
     1) Abraham/ ch. 4
     2) Adam/ ch. 5

27. C. Righteousness
      Imparted/ ch. 6, 7, 8
     1) Baptism
     2) The Slave Market
     3) Marriage

Lesson 4C
Paul's Missionary Strategy, and Ours
(Romans 10)

We have seen how this amazing man of God, Paul, had literally proclaimed fully the gospel all the way from Jerusalem to Illyricum (Rom. 15:19). He was, indeed, like a prisoner in Christ's victory procession, burning the victory incense, like the "fragrance of Christ", wherever he went (2 Cor. 2:14–16).

1. So as we look back over Paul's three missionary journeys, what stands out as absolutely **basic** to his whole strategy? And what does this teach us? Let's look again at what Paul said in his letter to the Romans. Read Romans 10:13–15.

   _____

   _____

   _____

2. Notice how literally Paul obeys the command of Jesus in Matthew 28:18–19 to **go**. Indeed this one word **go** becomes the basic principle in Paul's strategy of evangelism.

   How does Jesus further emphasize this principle in the example of the sower (Mark 4:3) and what does this teach us is essential for **our** evangelism?

   _____

   _____

3. Look again at what Paul says in Romans 10:13–15 where he explains the reason for this basic principle of evangelism, which is to GO.

   Why is it necessary to GO, according to these verses?

   _____

4. Now see what Paul says in Romans 15:20–21.

   Where did Paul seek to GO?

   _____

5. Paul **goes** to **sow** the word of the gospel where it has not been sown before. He follows Jesus in regarding the gospel as **seed** that is going to **grow**. Read what he says in 1 Corinthians 3:6.

   What two things must the agriculturalist do according to this verse, if their seed is to grow, and what do these two things represent in our sowing of the gospel?

   a) _____

   b) _____

   _____

6. Mark 1 Corinthians 3:6 in your Bible. We can see these two principles at work throughout all Paul's ministry. Look, for example, at his three year stay in Ephesus. **Turn to Acts 19 and 20.** Notice how Paul's evangelism was effective because he practiced

    • **continuous evangelism** and   • **continuous discipling.**

    Which of these, in bold print above, do we see principally in

    a) Acts 19:8–10?   _____

    b) Acts 20:20, 31–32?   _____

7. How can the effectiveness of Paul's strategy be seen in its impact on

    a) the growth of the church in and around Ephesus (Acts 19:10)?

        _____

        _____

    b) the spiritual atmosphere in Ephesus (Acts 19:11–20)?

        _____

        _____

    c) the social and religious atmosphere in Ephesus (Acts 19:21–41)?

        _____

        _____

8. We see therefore, how Paul's aim was to plant and train **local churches** that would practice **continuous evangelism** and **continuous discipling**. This leads (in Paul's day **and** in ours) to **effective growth in the church** and **effecting change in the community**. But finally, **who** were to engage in this double continuous ministry?

    Read what he later wrote to the church in Ephesus in Ephesians 4:12.

    _____

    _____

    _____

    Further Home Study

    Read and compare Paul's teaching on this in Ephesians 4:11–16; 1 Corinthians 12:12–30 and Romans 12:1–8.

9. How did Jesus teach exactly these same two principles of mission in Matthew 28:18–20? Mark these verses in your Bible.

    a) _____

    b) _____

    So absolutely basic to both Jesus' and Paul's missionary strategy was the need for

    A. continuous evangelism (sowing) and

    B. continuous discipling (watering).

We will now consider these in turn:

A. Need for Continuous EVANGELISM – Sowing

10. The "seed" Paul planted was, of course, the gospel message that he preached. Many Christians, however, feel they would be unable to share Christ with others in this way, as they feel **afraid**. In this they are not alone.

    a) How did Paul himself feel on this score? Read 1 Corinthians 2:1–5.

    _____

    b) But what did he do, in spite of these feelings? See also Romans 1:16.

    _____

    _____

11. A simple way to share this message today in continuous evangelism is by learning to use the SEAN evangelistic leaflet "How can I get to know God?". This is not a tract to be just handed out indiscriminately, but a powerful tool to help you explain the gospel clearly to someone and to help them to respond to Christ. Many people have already been led to Christ by ordinary Christians using this leaflet.

B. Need for Continuous DISCIPLING – Watering

12. As we have already seen, Paul knew that seed sown into the ground needs watering. Similarly, when a person responds to the gospel seed sown into their life, they need **training** and **discipling**. A **new** believer needs to be cared for, encouraged, taught in their new Christian life.

    Who was in charge of discipling the new believers in Corinth? Read 1 Corinthians 3:6.

    _____

13. So **continuous evangelism** needs to go hand in hand with **continuous discipling** to be effective. Paul undoubtedly used home-cell meetings for his **continuous discipling** (As the Jerusalem church had — Acts 2:46) to teach his converts those things that were "profitable" to them (see Acts 20:20). One method of discipling new believers, is the setting up of a **SEAN "Abundant Life" ("Life to the Full") Beginners' Group.**

14. Read again Jesus' words to us in Matthew 28:18–20 without comment; then let's pray together asking the Lord to help us to do something specific and practical about it.

15. After the Group Meeting, during the week, please do

    a) Test 4C, for this lesson.

    b) Lessons 5A and 5B with their tests. These tell us of Paul's exciting journey back from Corinth to Jerusalem and what awaited him there. Then do Lesson 5C.

Lesson 5A

To Jerusalem (Rendezvous in Troas)

Farewell to Ephesus (Acts 20:3–38)

A. Paul's Return to Philippi

Read Acts 20:3b–6.

1. So Paul's brief stay in Corinth passed happily and came to a quick end; he had been there a mere a) _____ months (Acts 20:3). Having sent his letter off to the Romans, Paul now got ready to return to his base church in Antioch, in the province of b) _____ (Acts 20:3).

2. But once again Paul was prevented in his plans by the hostile a) _____ (Acts 20:3) who now plotted to assassinate him. Perhaps on one dark night on the boat trip back to Syria they intended to throw him overboard. Anyway, Paul heard of their scheme, and thwarted it by a quick switch in his plans, going back instead to the province of b) _____ (Acts 20:3) where of course he revisited his beloved friends in the town of c) _____ (Acts 20:6).

3. On this rather roundabout journey via Macedonia back to Syria, Paul didn't travel alone. He was accompanied by a group of Christian men who seem to have been the representatives of the different Gentile churches that were sending "aid" with Paul to Jerusalem; they seemed to be acting as stewards.

   Using Acts 20:4, write in the church from which each representative came, and add the province if you can from your own knowledge.

	Church	Province
• Sopater	a) _____	b) _____
• Aristarchus and Secundus	c) _____	d) _____
• Gaius	e) _____	f) _____
• Tychicus (not given) and Trophimus (Acts 21:29)	g) _____	h) _____
• Timothy (not stated in verse, but look back to pictures in 1A.6)	i) _____	j) _____

4. So all the provinces where Paul had planted churches on his three missionary journeys were represented, except one, which was _____ (work this out from 5A.3 above).

Answers

1. a) 3
   b) Syria
2. a) Jews
   b) Macedonia
   c) Philippi

3. a) Berea
   b) Macedonia
   c) Thessalonica
   d) Macedonia
   e) Derbe

3. f) Galatia
   g) Ephesus
   h) Asia
   i) Lystra
   j) Galatia
4. Achaia

✐ **Note:** We don't know why the church in Corinth (Achaia) wasn't represented, but we know that they made a contribution toward this "aid" fund (Rom. 15:26).

5. Those of you who did Book 2 may remember how we saw that on the second missionary journey, when Paul left Philippi for the first time to go on to Thessalonica, Luke stayed behind in Philippi to help pastor the new church there. We know this because the **"we"** passage suddenly stopped. Now the "we" passage recommences as Paul gets back to Philippi again. In Acts 20:6, the writer doesn't say **"they"** sailed from Philippi, but a) "_____" sailed from Philippi, so we know that at this point the author of Acts, namely b) _____, rejoined Paul in his travels.

6. In spite of the joy of being reunited with Luke, a cloud of foreboding seemed to have settled on the party as in each city the Holy Spirit (probably through the lips of Christian prophets) had warned Paul that prison and troubles awaited him in a) _____ (Acts 20:22–23). However, to Paul, his own life was worth b) _____ (Acts 20:24); his only desire was to complete his c) _____ (Acts 20:24) that the Lord Jesus had given him to do.

7. From Philippi, Paul had sent the main party ahead of him to a) _____ (Acts 20:5), while he remained in Philippi to spend Passover week there with Luke. After which the two of them set sail together from Neapolis (the nearby port for Philippi). When they had crossed together from Troas to Europe six years previously, at the request of the Macedonian man in the vision, the journey had only taken two days (Acts 16:11); now the return crossing took them b) _____ days (Acts 20:6). So even the contrary winds seemed to echo the foreboding of the prophets that suffering and imprisonment awaited Paul in Jerusalem. However, eventually they all met up safely in c) _____ (Acts 20:6).

B. The Church in Troas

Read Acts 20:7–12.

8. When considering the churches Paul founded, somehow the church in Troas often seems to get left out. Yet many very important things happened in Troas although the church there was started on one of the most fleeting of Paul's visits. Following are five important points about this church which should also help you to review what we have already studied:

1) **First Visit to Troas on second missionary journey**

    Read Acts 16:8–10.

    It had been in Troas, on his **second** missionary journey, that Paul first met his great friend (who later wrote the Acts) the doctor called a) _____ (the start of the "we" passage tells us this).

Answers

5. a) "we"	6. a) Jerusalem	7. a) Troas
b) Luke	b) nothing	b) 5
	c) task	c) Troas
		8. a) Luke

It was also in Troas (on the same occasion) that Paul had his vision of the man from b) _____ (Acts 16:8–9); and it was from Troas that he launched out on his mission to the continent of Europe (Macedonia) where he left Luke in Philippi as we have just seen.

2) Second visit to Troas on third missionary journey

Read 2 Corinthians 2:12–13 and review Lesson 3A.16 and 17.

Paul also paid a fleeting visit to Troas on his journey from Ephesus to Philippi. It was here that he waited patiently for his colleague, called c) _____, who was to have come with news of the situation in Corinth.

In spite of his deep concern to get news from the trouble-stricken church in Corinth (through Titus), Paul preached the Good News about Christ in Troas and soon found that the Lord had d) _____ (2 Cor. 2:12) a door for the work there, as many people became Christians.

In recalling those days in Troas, Paul bursts out in his cry of joy in 2 Corinthians 2:14, *"Thanks be to God, who... uses us to spread the aroma of the knowledge of him (Christ)* e) _____ *"* (in his triumphal procession – look back to the picture in Lesson 3C.9).

3) Third visit to Troas (also on third missionary journey)

Read Acts 20:6–12. Now he was back in Troas we see how amazingly the church had developed, the fruit of just a very brief period of ministry.

First the upper room where they met was so crammed with people that the young man, called f) _____ (v.9), had to wedge himself into a g) _____. We can see, too, that they needed many h) _____ (v.8) to meet the needs of all the people.

They were so eager to hear all Paul could teach them that they were willing to listen to him all i) _____ long (vv.7, 11).

They also had met together to break j) _____ (v.11), that is, to celebrate the Lord's Supper, together. **This is the only one of Paul's churches where this is specifically recorded** (although Paul teaches about it in 1 Corinthians 11:17–34).

On this occasion he was able to stay there k) _____ days (v.6). The farewell gathering was memorable for the miracle Paul performed in raising l) _____ (vv.9–12) from the dead.

🖋 **Note:** Eutychus had probably been working hard all day. During Paul's long address, and as a result of the stuffy atmosphere caused by the crowded room and the many lamps, he fell asleep from sheer exhaustion, just like Jesus in the boat. He had wedged himself on to a third storey windowsill. Suddenly he fell with a thud to the pavement of the street below, and when they picked him up he was dead. When Paul raised him

Answers

8. b) Macedonia
   c) Titus
   d) opened
   e) everywhere

8. f) Eutychus
   g) window
   h) lamps
   i) night

8. j) bread
   k) seven
   l) Eutychus

from the dead it caused a tremendous sensation: and on this wave of rejoicing and loving fellowship the missionary team continued on its way.

4) Final Visit to Troas (On release from first imprisonment)

Read 2 Timothy 4:13.

Years later, when Paul wrote his last letter (2 Timothy) before his death as a martyr, we know that he had been back to visit the church in Troas because he had left his m) _____ and his n) _____ there (2 Tim. 4:13).

5) Troas in Times of Ignatius

The church in Troas was still flourishing in the time of Ignatius (a Christian leader of the 2nd century, after all the apostles were dead). So Troas was one of Paul's success churches in every way.

9. **Review** by writing in the letter of the picture that matches each event.

			Picture
1)	Met Luke, vision of Macedonian.	2nd journey.	_____
2)	Waited in vain for Titus.	3rd journey – on way **to** Macedonia and Achaia.	_____
3)	Raised boy who fell from window.	3rd journey – return **from** Achaia and Macedonia.	_____
4)	Left cloak and scrolls.	After release from 1st imprisonment.	_____
5)	Still flourishing in time of Ignatius.	Next century.	_____

Answers

8. m) cloak
   n) scrolls

9. 1) A
   2) B
   3) C
   4) D
   5) E

C. Paul's Journey from Troas to Miletus

10. Read Acts 20:13–17, following each step of the journey from Troas to Miletus on this map. As Paul was anxious to get to Jerusalem by the day of a) _____ (Acts 20:16) he decided to take a boat, even though it was not calling at b) _____ (v.16). Actually Paul sent off his companions on this boat, while he himself walked the 30 miles overland from Troas, letter on map c) _____, to the next port called d) _____ marked by letter e) _____ on map.

It was most unusual for Paul to travel alone like this and no doubt he did it this time in order to have quiet with the Lord. In view of the repeated warnings of trouble ahead he wanted guidance as to whether or not he should go up to f) _____ (Acts 20:22–23).

Was the Lord wanting him to go directly to **Rome** instead? At Assos Paul joined the boat, having walked the 30 miles in a day: not bad for a man of about 57 years of age!!

11. The sea trip must have been beautiful beyond imagination as they called at ports on three of the lovely Aegean islands. These were a) _____, letter b) _____, c) _____, letter d) _____ and e) _____, letter f) _____. Finally they docked on the mainland at g) _____, letter h) _____, having sailed right past i) _____, letter j) _____.

12. From Miletus, Paul sent a messenger on the 50 mile journey to a) _____ (Acts 20:17), to let the b) _____ (Acts 20:17) there know of his arrival. They immediately hurried over to Miletus to see Paul before his boat sailed (look back to the picture in the Introductory Group Study, Frame 3).

D. Paul's Farewell Message to the Elders of Ephesus

13. In this message Paul speaks of the **past**, the **present** and the **future**.

The Past: Read Acts 20:17–21 and 33–35.

Review Lesson 1B, Frames 5 to 7 and Pictures A and B in Frame 1.

Answers

10. a) Pentecost	11. a) Mitylene	11. g) Miletus
b) Ephesus	b) Y	h) L
c) G	c) Chios	i) Ephesus
d) Assos	d) X	j) P
e) Q	e) Samos	12. a) Ephesus
f) Jerusalem	f) Z	b) elders

The Present: Read Acts 20:22–26

Paul tells them (as we saw in Frame 6) how in every city, the Holy Spirit warned him that prison and troubles awaited him in a) _____ (Acts 20:22–23).

The Future: Read Acts 20:26–32

Paul warns them that after he had left, the Christian flock would be attacked by savage b) _____ (Acts 20:29) i.e. false teachers. Therefore as shepherds of the church he calls them to keep watch over themselves and the flock.

14. **To Think and Pray About**

    Look thoughtfully through Paul's farewell message to the Ephesian elders in Acts 20:17–38 listing the principles of ministry that emerge from his example. Then pray that each may be sharpened in your own ministry.

15. The time of sailing was near. Paul knelt with them and prayed. They were all deeply moved, especially because Paul had said they would never a) _____ (Acts 20:38) him again (although in this it seems that he was mistaken, as we shall see later). They accompanied him to the port and as the ship slipped out of sight round the great marble lions that marked the headland of this majestic harbor, they all b) _____ (v.37).

16. Now review and then do Test 5A.

Answers

13. a) Jerusalem
    b) wolves

15. a) see
    b) wept

Lesson 5B

Arrest in Jerusalem

Eyes on Rome (Acts 21:1–23)

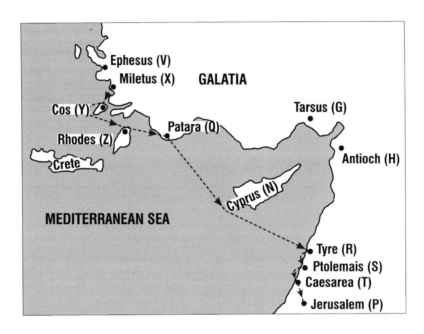

✎ **Note:** In this lesson, whenever there is no reference after the question, find the answer in the passage given for that section.

A. Paul's Journey from Miletus to Jerusalem (Acts 21:1–16)

1. Read Acts 21:1–2 and use the above map to answer.

    Having wrenched themselves away from the Ephesian elders at Miletus, they sailed by two islands, called a) _____, letter b) _____ and c) _____, letter d) _____; and finally reached the mainland again at e) _____, letter f) _____, where they had to change ships for one running across the Mediterranean to Syria.

2. Read Acts 21:3–6.

    They sailed south of the island of a) _____, letter b) _____. This must have brought back happy memories to Paul of his very first missionary activity, on his **first** journey, on his way out to Galatia.

Answers

1. a) Cos
    b) Y
    c) Rhodes
    d) Z
    e) Patara
    f) Q

2. a) Cyprus
    b) N

SEAN – Study by Extension for All Nations

3. Then they made straight for the city of a) _____ in Syria, letter b) _____, where the ship stayed in port a week, unloading its cargo. Here the believers urged Paul **not** to go to c) _____; Luke tells us that they said this in the power of the d) _____ _____.

4. Read Acts 21:7.

    At the next port the ship only stopped a day. This was a) _____, letter b) _____; but again they spent the time profitably with the believers there.

5. Read Acts 21:8–14.

    At last they arrived at their port of disembarkation, that was a) _____, letter b) _____, where they were taken to the house of one of the original seven men chosen to serve in the church in Jerusalem (Acts 6:3–5); his name was c) _____, and he had four d) _____ who proclaimed God's message (prophesied). After several days, here once more Paul was warned of persecutions in Jerusalem, this time by a prophet called e) _____ who as a sign took Paul's f) _____ and tied his own hands and feet with it. But Paul said he was willing, not only to be bound, but also to g) _____ for Jesus; so they pressed on to Jerusalem, letter h) _____.

    ## B. In Jerusalem (Read Acts 21:17–26)

6. Finally, the great day dawned when Paul could fulfill his long ambition to hand over personally the a) _____ (Rom. 15:26) from the Gentile churches to the poor among God's people in Jerusalem. However, reading between the lines it all seems to have been something of an anticlimax. Certainly, the b) _____ welcomed them warmly (Acts 21:17), and the following day Luke says, *"Paul and the rest of us (that is, the delegates who had brought the offering) went to see* c) _____" (Acts 21:18). All the church d) _____ were also present (Acts 21:18). So this was obviously the official meeting for the handing over of the "aid". Paul gave a complete report of everything that God had done among the e) _____ (Acts 21:19). But, as one commentator says: "The reaction was disappointing. The elders made appropriate noises of praise to God and turned promptly to a much more pressing affair".

7. James and the elders urged Paul to make a public gesture of submission to the Jewish law by joining four other Jews who had made a vow, paying their expenses to have their heads shaved, and entering the Temple with them where an a) _____ (Acts 21:26b) would be made for them! This way, they said, the Jews would see that the rumors about Paul's preaching and teaching were false and that he lived in obedience to the law.

    So this was to be the result of his trip to Jerusalem, against which the b) _____ (Acts 21:4) had consistently warned him.

    ## Answers

3.		5.		6.	
a)	Tyre	a)	Caesarea	a)	contribution
b)	R	b)	T	b)	brothers/ believers
c)	Jerusalem	c)	Philip	c)	James
d)	Holy Spirit	d)	daughters	d)	elders
4.		e)	Agabus	e)	Gentiles
a)	Ptolemais	f)	belt	7.	
b)	S	g)	die	a)	offering
		h)	P	b)	Spirit

> *Unhappily, far from achieving its end, Paul's action in the temple was an absolute debacle.*

C. The Jews Attempt to Kill Paul (Acts 21:27–36)

Read what happened in Acts 21:27–36

8. Some Jews from the province of a) _____ (Acts 21:27) had seen Paul with b) _____ (Acts 21:29), the Gentile delegate from c) _____ (Acts 21:29), and thought Paul had brought him into the Temple. They stirred up the crowd to seize d) _____ (Acts 21:27). Pandemonium broke out, and had it not been for the swift intervention of the Roman e) _____ (Acts 21:31–32), Paul would have been killed on the spot. He rushed into the rioting mob and carried Paul to the security of the Roman f) _____ (Acts 21:34) (Fort of Antonia) which overlooked the Temple area at that time.

9. On the steps, leading up into the fort, Paul asked and received permission from the commander to speak to the crowd (If you have done Book 1, look back to the picture in Lesson 1A.2 in that Book). The crowd hushed, when Paul spoke to them in their own language, which was _____ (Acts 22:2). Paul gave his testimony.

D. Paul's Defense and Testimony before the Mob (Acts 22:3–23)

Read Paul's testimony in Acts 22:3–21. It will provide an excellent review of all you learned in Book 1!

10. The crowd listened quietly to Paul's testimony until he mentioned his call to the a) _____ (Acts 22:21–22). Then their screams of fury forced the Roman commander to take Paul into the b) _____ (Acts 22:24) where he ordered his men to c) _____ him (Acts 22:24) as a torture to force a confession of guilt from him. Paul appealed against this as unlawful, on the grounds that he was a d) _____ citizen (Acts 22:25).

You may remember that Paul had this citizenship passed on to him from his father (who must have received it for some outstanding service rendered to the Empire). In this Paul was one step ahead of the commander himself who had paid a e) _____ of _____ for his citizenship (Acts 22:28).

Answers

8. a) Asia
    b) Trophimus
    c) Ephesus
    d) Paul
    e) commander
    f) barracks

9. Aramaic

10. a) Gentiles
    b) barracks
    c) flog
    d) Roman
    e) lot/ money

11. The commander was really shaken by this, and the next day he _____ Paul (had his chains taken off) (Acts 22:30).

E. Paul and the Earthly High Priest (Read Acts 23:1–10)

12. Still anxious to get to the bottom of the matter the commander took Paul to stand before the Sanhedrin to find out what they held against him. Paul had scarcely started to speak when a man struck him on the mouth, having been ordered to do this by the a) _____ _____, called b) _____ (Acts 23:2). Paul, enraged by this indignity, called him a c) _____ _____ (Acts 23:3), apparently not realizing he was the high priest.

13. Paul knew that the council was made up of two rival religious parties: his old party the Pharisees, who believed in the resurrection, and the a) _____ (Acts 23:6) who didn't, to which party the high priest belonged! So Paul, determined to establish his position, cried out, "*I am a* b) _____, *descended from* c) _____. *I stand on trial because of the hope of the* d) _____ *of the dead*" (Acts 23:6). Immediately a e) _____ broke out (Acts 23:7), the Pharisees defending Paul against the Sadducees and the high priest! The Roman soldiers saved Paul from being torn to pieces by taking him back to the fort, leaving the council in uproar behind them!

F. Paul and the Heavenly High Priest (Read Acts 23:11)

14. The following night the a) _____ stood by Paul and said, "*As you have testified about me in* b) _____, *so you must also testify in* c) _____" (Acts 23:11)!

15. At this moment, perhaps as never before, Paul must have realized who his high priest really was; one who had gone into the very presence of God, that is, a) _____, the Son of God (Heb. 4:14); a high priest who is b) _____ (Heb. 7:26). Unlike all earthly high priests, who needed to sacrifice every day for their own c) _____ (Heb. 7:27), he is the Son, who has been made d) _____ for ever (Heb. 7:28). This was a high priest who could feel e) _____ for Paul's f) _____ (Heb. 4:15). Indeed he came to Paul in his moment of extreme weakness and need with a word of encouragement, saying: "*Take* g) _____" (Acts 23:11). How different from the earthly high priest who had ordered someone to strike Paul on the h) _____ (Acts 23:2). It was just as if new light burst into Paul's weary soul as he realized that this high priest could help those who are i) _____ (Heb. 2:18), because he himself was j) _____ (Heb. 2:18) and yet without k) _____ (Heb. 4:15).

Answers

11. released	b) Pharisee	b) Jerusalem	f) weaknesses
12. a) high priest	c) Pharisees	c) Rome	g) courage
b) Ananias	d) resurrection	15. a) Jesus	h) mouth
c) whitewashed wall	e) dispute	b) holy	i) tempted
13. a) Sadducees	14. a) Lord	c) sins	j) tempted
		d) perfect	k) sin
		15. e) empathy	16. a) A

16. **To Think About**

Read Hebrews 7:26–28. Notice how the teaching in Hebrews about the high priest perfectly expresses what Paul experienced on this occasion: first with Ananias, then with the risen Lord Jesus. Look carefully at the drawings below. That blow on the mouth must have revealed to him afresh the utter barrenness of the earthly high priest; a sinner like all other men, Picture a) _____. Then, as Jesus came to him he must have realized as never before that Jesus alone was his perfect high priest, Picture b) _____.

What does this passage mean to you? Pray about this.

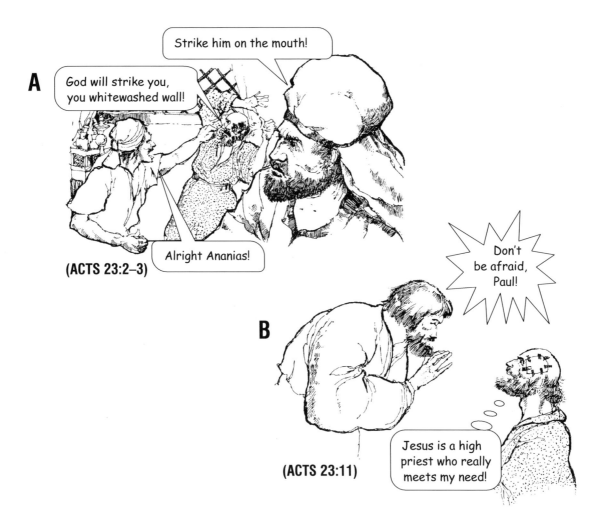

17. Now review and then do Test 5B.

Answers

b) B

Lesson 5C

Paul's Love for Jew and Gentile

(Romans, Chapters 9 to 11)

1. Jesus said (and it is one of his harder sayings):

   "Love your enemies, and pray for those who persecute you." (Matt. 5:44)

   If ever a man had enemies who hated him it was Paul. His own people, the Jews, never ceased their ruthless persecution of him. What example of this happened in

   a) Corinth (Acts 20:3)?

   _____

   b) Jerusalem (Acts 21:30–32)?

   _____

2. What was at the heart of this bitter Jewish persecution of Paul?

   Read Acts 22:21–22.

   _____

3. How then did Paul cope with this real life situation? Could he actually *love* these vicious opponents even as Jesus, his Master, had done before him?

   Romans allows us to peer into the recesses of Paul's mind and heart, to see something of this inner struggle. Remember that he was in **Corinth**, the very place where the assassination plot was being hatched up, even as he wrote these words!

   Read Romans 1:16; 2:9–10, 24; 3:1–2, 9, 29–30.

   What is the recurring theme in these verses? And what is Paul trying to stress throughout?

   _____

   _____

4. However, it is in chapters 9 to 11 that Paul really brings his teaching on the Jews to a head. To get a glimpse of this, read the opening verses of these three chapters, as given below, and in each case try to say how Paul reflects Christ's love.

   a) **Chapter 9**, verses 1 to 3 (Compare Galatians 3:13)

   _____

   b) **Chapter 10**, verse 1 (Compare Matthew 5:44)

   _____

   c) **Chapter 11**, verses 1 to 5

   _____

5. In chapters 9 and 10 Paul explains to the Jews, who found it so difficult to accept the Gentiles, that a **sovereign** God has a perfect right to choose whom he will, Jew or Gentile, and he supports this with arguments from their own Scriptures. Read Romans 9:14–18.

    What illustration does Paul use to explain the sovereignty of God in Romans 9:19–21?

    _____

6. Of course, God's sovereignty differs from all human sovereignty in two points: it is both **perfect and all-loving**. Without understanding this, Paul's teaching here could appear to be harsh; with a closer look we see that it is the exact opposite! Remember, for example, that the Jews were accusing God of being too **lenient** because he was accepting the Godless Gentiles into his kingdom. So Paul is not arguing here that, as Sovereign, God has a perfect right to be **harsh** with sinners, but that he has a perfect right to be **lenient** with them! This was the disputed point!

    How does Paul show that even in the Old Testament this was the kind of sovereignty that God showed? Read Romans 9:23–26.

    _____

    _____

7. So with this kind of insight into the sovereignty of God, Paul bursts out (in chapter 10) into a plea for more evangelists who will go into all the world with the message of salvation (as we saw in last week's Group Study on this chapter). Notice how in chapter 10, in contrast to chapter 9, Paul lays heavy stress on humanity's response and responsibility. Read again Romans 10:15. Then see how Paul quotes Isaiah to support his plea. To whom is Isaiah referring in Romans 10:20?

    _____

8. Indeed, Paul could accept the bitter hostility of the Jews because he could see that God, in his sovereignty, had used even this to forward his purposes of love. Nowhere is this set forth more clearly than in Romans, chapter 11, the **key chapter** on the **Jews**.

    a) What good thing did Paul see coming out of the unbelief and enmity of the Jews in Romans 11:11–12?

        _____

        _____

    b) How did this work out when Paul was in Ephesus (Acts 19:8–10)?

        _____

        _____

        _____

9. What illustration does Paul use to explain how the enmity of the Jews would, in God's sovereignty, result in this **double** blessing, to both **Gentile and Jew**? Read Romans 11:16b.–24. Discuss what each part of the illustration means.

    _____

10. Read Paul's comments in Romans 11:25–36. What an example of loving one's enemies!

   In what modern situations can we follow Paul's example of Christ-like love toward our enemies? Read what he says in Romans 12:14, 17–21.

   _____

   _____

   _____

11. So we can see that perhaps one of the most remarkable facets of the glittering and multisided genius of Paul, the apostle to the **Gentiles**, was his deep-seated concern for the well-being of the **Jew**, and this in spite of all they had done to ruin his work in every place. We can see his great **love** for them expressed in the following two ways:

   A. His letter to the Romans in which he laments their unbelief and is willing even to fall under God's curse if this could bring them to faith. He also reaffirms his firm belief that, in God's ultimate plan, the Jewish nation will be gathered in as true believers in their Messiah!

   B. The practical help from his Gentile churches which he insisted on carrying personally to the poor in Jerusalem, **in spite of** the extreme danger and of his overwhelming urge to go to Rome, and from there to Spain.

   Paul's extraordinary **love** for his **enemies** springs, of course, from the **love** God showed to him on the Damascus road. If we are to experience this kind of outgoing **love** it can only come from the same source.

   We will pray together after reading (without comment) about this in

   • Romans 5:7–8 and 10.

   • Romans 8:35–39.

13. After the Group Meeting, during the week, please do

   a) Test 5C, for this lesson.

   b) Lessons 6A and 6B, with their tests. These tell how Paul did go to **Rome** after visiting Jerusalem, but in a way far different from that planned!

   c) Then do Lesson 6C.

Lesson 6A

Captive in Caesarea: En Route to Rome

(Acts 23:12 to 26:24)

1. We now come to Paul's first prolonged period of captivity, which, for such an active man, must have been most frustrating. This took place on the Mediterranean coast, in the important seaside port of **Caesarea**, and dragged on for more than ____ years (Acts 24:27).

*But wait a minute! We remember that Paul had disembarked in Caesarea, but had then gone up to Jerusalem. Why then have we suddenly jumped back to Caesarea? Well, its unlikely that even Agabus could have imagined that his prophecy in Caesarea, that Paul would be bound (Acts 21:10–11), could have had quite such an immediate and startling fulfillment. The truth is that **within two weeks** Paul was back again in Caesarea, and bound as a prisoner! How did this happen?*

How Paul Got Back to Caesarea (Acts 23:12–35)

2. Let's go back to Acts 23:11–15 when Paul was still in Jerusalem and read what happened there. As you read, recall Paul's love for these Jews that we saw in Romans chapters 9 to 11.

   It all started the morning after Paul's encounters, first with Ananias and then with Jesus (the human and the spiritual high priests). Some Jewish conspirators took a vow that they wouldn't a) _____ or _____ until they had b) _____ Paul. In all, there were more than c) ____ of these conspirators.

3. Read in Acts 23:16–22 how their plan was thwarted.

   Their plot was overheard by Paul's a) _____ who immediately went to the Roman fort of Antonia to report it to Paul who told him to take this news to the Roman commander, whose name was b) _____ _____. (You will find his name in Acts 23:26, at the start of the letter he wrote.)

Answers

1. 2	2. a) eat/ drink b) killed c) 40	3. a) nephew b) Claudius Lysias

---

SEAN – Study by Extension for All Nations

4.   Read in Acts 23:23–24 how Lysias reacted to this news.

Lysias acted with the utmost speed and efficiency; that same night he sent Paul to Caesarea, heavily escorted by an armed guard which consisted of

Number	**Description**
a) _____	b) _____
c) _____	d) _____
e) _____	f) _____

He also sent a covering letter explaining his action to the Roman governor in Caesarea, whose name was g) _____ (Acts 23:26).

5.   Now read what Lysias said in his letter, in Acts 23:26–30. We ought to take special note of two important points mentioned in this letter because they altered the whole conditions of Paul's stay in Caesarea and onwards. First, he informed Felix that Paul was a a) _____ _____ (Acts 23:27). Secondly, he clearly said that, as far as the Roman law was concerned, b) _____ _____ could be brought against Paul (Acts 23:29). These facts led to Paul being held under **light** arrest while he was in Caesarea, which meant that he could always see his c) _____ (Acts 24:23).

6.   Read Acts 23:31–35. Once they were clear of the danger zone, the a) _____ all returned to their base in Jerusalem, while the b) _____ continued on with Paul to Caesarea, where they delivered over Paul and the accompanying letter to the governor called c) _____.

7.   Paul himself tells us that from the time he left Caesarea for Jerusalem, after Agabus' prophecy that he would be bound there, to the time he returned as a prisoner to Caesarea, was only _____ days (Acts 24:11). As Luke and Aristarchus were with Paul later, they probably followed him to Caesarea to be there at his trial. Now read the description of Caesarea in the following box.

> Caesarea was a truly magnificent city, which had been built on the Mediterranean coast, about 65 miles north west of Jerusalem, by Herod the Great (puppet Jewish king in Palestine when Jesus was born). It had a marvellous harbor where Paul had disembarked on returning from both his second and third missionary journeys (Acts 18:22 and 21:8). It had extravagant palaces, a really enormous amphitheatre for the Roman games, and a huge temple dedicated to Caesar and to Rome. It was the capital city of the Roman province of Judea (which now included the Samaria of Jesus' day) and was therefore the residence of the Roman governors and of the reigning Herod in Palestine. Look back to the map on the Title Page of Lesson 5B and make sure you know the position of Caesarea.

Answers

4.	a) 200	5.	a) Roman citizen	6.	a) soldiers
	b) soldiers		b) no charge		b) cavalry
	c) 70		c) friends		c) Felix
	d) horsemen			7.	12
	e) 200				
	f) spearmen				
	g) Felix				

8. First let's just run over the different events that Luke has recorded for us as happening in this great city. About 20 years previously, it was in Caesarea that a Roman army captain had been converted under Peter's ministry; his name was a) _____ (Acts 10:24). Just before this a colleague of the martyr Stephen had arrived in Caesarea, fresh from his successful mission in Samaria and from the conversion of the Ethiopian official in the desert; his name was b) _____ (Acts 8:40). Even more important, we know that this man was still living in Caesarea at this time and that it was in his house that Paul and the others had stayed, on their way through to Jerusalem (Acts 21:8) Remember that he now had four grown up unmarried c) _____ (Acts 21:9) who took an active part in the ministry in Caesarea by d) _____ (Acts 21:9). Obviously this man was a leader of the church in Caesarea and Paul and his colleagues, Luke and Aristarchus, must have spent lots of time with him and his dedicated family during those two years there because, remember, Paul was allowed to see his e) _____ (Acts 24:23).

9. So it was to this city and to this church that Paul came, probably in the middle of the year 57 A.D. (We will see shortly how we know the year by the date of what happened two years later.) Therefore, according to our way of reckoning Paul's age (see the note at the foot of Supplement 1), he must have been about _____ years old at the time when, as a prisoner, he arrived in Caesarea.

10. The missionary team seem to have been engaged in two main ministries while they were in Caesarea:

   A. Paul had a remarkable evangelistic ministry to the authorities who were ruling in Palestine.

   B. Luke, almost certainly encouraged and assisted by Paul, seems to have done a lot of research in preparation for writing the third Gospel (Luke's Gospel).

   By glancing through Luke's description in Acts, chapters 24 to 26, we can see that Luke describes in detail just one of these kinds of ministry (A and B) given above, that is ministry a) _____.

   In his usual modest way, Luke passes over entirely any mention of his own research program which we believe he must have engaged in during this period, which was ministry b) _____.

   For the rest of this lesson we will consider these two aspects of their ministry.

A. Paul's Witness to the "Great" of this World

11. Luke describes in detail how Paul testified with considerable power to three of the top authorities in Palestine, both Roman and Jewish, and in two cases before their women as well.

Answers

8. a) Cornelius	9. 57	
b) Philip	10. a) A	
c) daughters	b) B	
d) prophesying		
e) friends		

These authorities were

a) _____ (Roman governor) and his wife b) _____ (Acts 24:24);
c) _____ (Roman governor) (Acts 25:6); d) _____ (Jewish king)
and his sister e) _____ (Acts 25:23).

12. **Exercise**

It will help you to remember Paul's encounters with these five different authorities if you mark them in your Bible in the following way:

1. Put a ring round "Felix" in Acts 24:2, then put "1" in the margin.
   Put a ring round "Drusilla" in Acts 24:24, and then put "2" in the margin.

2. Put a ring round "Festus" in Acts 25:1 and write "3" in the margin.

3. Put a ring round "Agrippa" and "Bernice" in Acts 25:13 and write "4/5" in the margin.

When you have time, read the remarkable accounts of Paul's faithful and fearless testimony before these different "great ones", in chapters 24 and 25. We will only point out the main things that happened.

1. **Felix (and Drusilla) — Acts 24:1–27**

13. **Historical note:**

Felix, the Roman governor, was a most unsavory character, always on the look out for bribes. He had been born a slave but had risen to power thanks to his brother's influence with the Emperor Claudius. One Roman writer said of him, "He wields the power of a king with the mind of a slave". Within a few months a terrible riot broke out in Caesarea and Felix was recalled to Rome, stripped of his position, and only narrowly escaped execution (thanks to his brother's intervention). This took place in 59 A.D. — so this is how we can fix the date with reasonable accuracy.

Drusilla, his wife, was from the Herod family, and had been seduced by Felix in her youth to divorce her husband and come and live with him as his third wife.

This, then, was the man who sat in judgment over the great apostle Paul! As you can see from your marked Bible, Luke tells how Paul witnessed publicly before him on two occasions:

First, without his wife being present, on the occasion when the lawyer called
a) _____ (Acts 24:2) laid his accusations against Paul, on behalf of Ananias the high priest.

Answers

11. a) Felix
    b) Drusilla
    c) Festus
    d) Agrippa
    e) Bernice

13. a) Tertullus

Second, when his wife b) _____ (Acts 24:24) was also present, and Paul spoke with such power about righteousness, self-control and the coming day of c) _____ (Acts 24:25), that Felix was so shaken that he said he would d) _____ _____ him again (Acts 24:25). Indeed he often e) _____ with Paul (Acts 24:26) although he also hoped in this way to get Paul to offer him a f) _____ , in order to get free. However, as we can see from the historical note above, within a few months he was recalled to g) _____. He was replaced by:

2. Festus — Acts 25:1–12

14. **Historical note:**

Festus, was a man of higher principles than Felix, although still willing to compromise in order to please the Jews and in that way to avoid trouble in his province. Within two years he was dead. With this change from Felix to Festus events took a new turn. Although Festus was well aware of Paul's innocence he decided to please the Jews by sending Paul back to a) _____ for trial (Acts 25:9). Knowing that this would have meant certain death, Paul took a very bold step and appealed to the Emperor, b) _____ (Acts 25:10–11). As a Roman citizen Paul had the right to be tried in Rome, and it was this right that he now demanded and that was granted by c) _____ (Acts 25:12).

3. Agrippa (the second) (and Bernice) — Acts 25:13 to 26:32

15. **Historical note:**

Agrippa was the current member of the Herod family ruling over the territory that had been under Philip the Tetrarch. He also had a palace in Caesarea. He was the brother of Drusilla (wife of the deposed Felix) and of

Bernice, with whom he lived (causing some scandal). As all the Herods, he was only half Jewish.

Poor Festus was now in a real fix, with a prisoner on his hands to send to Caesar, and yet without knowing what a) _____ (Acts 25:27) to level against him! Now it so happened that at this time the Jewish king returned to his residence in Caesarea; his name was b) _____ (Acts 25:13). Perhaps, thought Festus, he will understand the accusations that the Jews are making against Paul. And so he asked Agrippa if he would help.

16. With his witness before this royal couple, Paul's ministry to the great of this world reached its peak, for not only were the king and his sister present, that is a) _____ and b) _____ but also all the high ranking c) _____ (Acts 25:23) and leading men of the d) _____ (Acts 25:23) and, of course, the Roman governor himself, that is e) _____ (Acts 25:23). What an array of dignitaries before whom to preach!

Answers

13. b) Drusilla
    c) judgment
    d) send for
    e) talked
    f) bribe
    g) Rome

14. a) Jerusalem
    b) Caesar
    c) Festus
15. a) charges
    b) Agrippa

16. a) Agrippa
    b) Bernice
    c) officers
    d) city
    e) Festus

17. Paul welcomed this glorious opportunity! Read his fearless testimony in Acts 26:2–23. With great courage, vigor, and clarity he first told them how he had once been a strict a) _____ (Acts 26:5) who had persecuted the followers of Jesus of Nazareth in an attempt to make them deny their faith and b) _____ (Acts 26:11). Then one eventful day his whole life had been turned upside down when he met Jesus on the road to Damascus. From that moment he had not been c) _____ to the vision from heaven (Acts 26:19) and hadn't ceased to give his witness to both small and d) _____ alike (Acts 26:22). And what a crowd of great ones were listening to his amazing testimony now!

18. Suddenly Paul was interrupted by someone shouting at him! Read what happened in Acts 26:24–32. The person who interrupted him was a) _____ who shouted out that he was b) _____ (Acts 26:24)! But the things Paul was saying were c) _____ and _____ (Acts 26:25); they were events which had actually happened to him and which alone could have changed him from a merciless Pharisee into a love-filled Christian, and many of those present must have realized this for, as Paul said, these things had not happened in a d) _____ (Acts 26:26).

19. Then looking the king straight in the eyes, Paul addressed him personally: *"King a) _____ , do you believe the b) _____? I know you do"* (Acts 26:27). For a moment there must have been a stunned silence at Paul's audacity in so addressing a monarch while the king struggled with his protesting conscience. Then, in a desperate effort to wriggle out of his embarrassment he sneered: *"Do you think that in such a short time you can persuade me to be a c) _____?"* (Acts 26:28).

   But as the assembly rose, Agrippa said to Festus *"This man could have been d) _____ _____ if he had not appealed to Caesar"* (Acts 26:32). It was a sad ending; but Paul had once more been faithful to his Master, and who knows how many, in that glittering crowd of top society, might have responded in the secret of their hearts: "Yes, Paul, I **do** believe and I too receive him as my Lord and Savior, even as you did".

B. Research for Writing the Third Gospel

20. By now you will be used to Luke's modest method of writing: always highlighting Paul's ministry; never mentioning his own. What an example to us! But it means that, unless we read carefully between the lines, we can easily miss half of the missionary team's ministry. In this final section we try and see that we don't fall into that trap.

Answers

17. a) Pharisee
    b) blaspheme
    c) disobedient
    d) great

18. a) Festus
    b) insane
    c) true/ reasonable
    d) corner

19. a) Agrippa
    b) prophets
    c) Christian
    d) set free

🖉 **Note:** For the reasons given above, nothing in this section is certain. However, the strong indirect evidence makes it all highly probable. Read this evidence in the following box.

> At the beginning of his Gospel Luke says that he had carefully investigated all the things he wrote about Jesus (Luke 1:3), so when did he have the opportunity to do this research? We know that up till now he had been away from Palestine on the missionary journeys with Paul. Once they left Caesarea for Rome he apparently did not return to Palestine. So he must have made his fact-finding journeys throughout Palestine during this period of two years when they had their base in Caesarea.

It is generally accepted that during these visits he must have had long talks with Mary, the mother of Jesus: how else could he have known the things that she remembered and a) _____ deeply about (Luke 2:19)? In this way she would have confided in him, a doctor, the intimate and miraculous details about Jesus' birth: that she, being a b) _____ (Luke 1:27, 34) had conceived by the c) _____ _____ (Luke 1:35) coming upon her.

21. Who else but Mary could have told him the story of how Jesus as a little boy had got lost in Jerusalem, and how they had eventually found him in the a) _____ (Luke 2:46) where the Jewish teachers were amazed at his understanding and b) _____ (Luke 2:47)? How else could Luke have known that Mary treasured all these things in the secret of her c) _____ (Luke 2:51)?

22. It is well known that Luke stresses the place and ministry of women in his Gospel. Could he have been alerted to the women's point of view by Philip's four a) _____ (Acts 21:9) who, he is quick to report, were so active in proclaiming God's message? After all, they also lived in b) _____ (Acts 21:8) where Luke was based at this time.

23. Again Luke gives a special place to the "Samaritans" in his Gospel. Remember that it was Philip who years before had gone to the principal city in a) _____ (Acts 8:5) and preached Jesus with such power that many b) _____ his message (Acts 8:12); so he had started the church there. Remember, Philip also now lived in Caesarea!

24. It is also probable that he was assisted by the Lord's brother, _____, whom he had met in Jerusalem (Acts 21:18), who would have told him about Jesus' youth and earthly ministry.

Study the following map carefully to see what possible route Luke may have taken to gather his information.

Answers		

20. a) pondered
  b) virgin
  c) Holy Spirit
21. a) temple
  b) answers
  c) heart
	22. a) daughters
	  b) Caesarea
	23. a) Samaria
	  b) believed
		24. James

MAP OF PALESTINE

Reconstruction of possible route taken by Luke
on his fact-finding tour from Caesarea

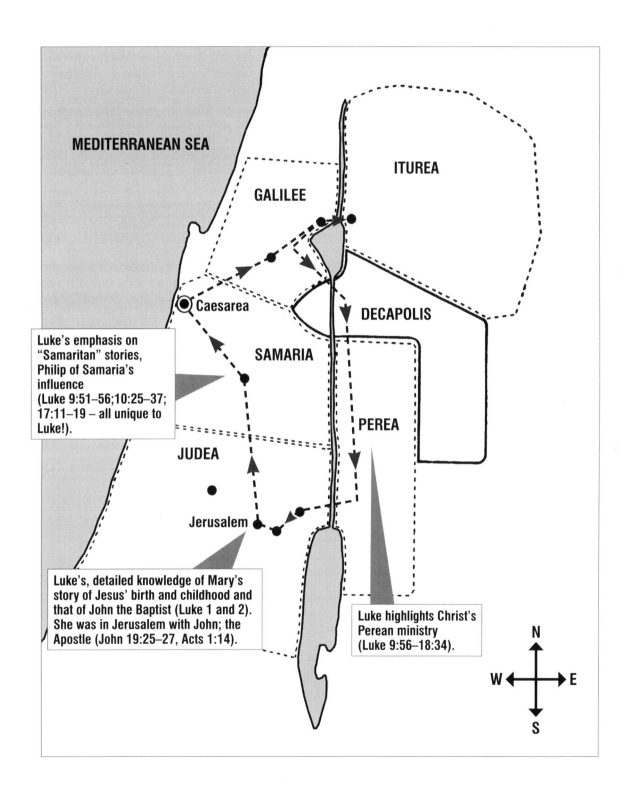

MEDITERRANEAN SEA

ITUREA

GALILEE

Caesarea

DECAPOLIS

SAMARIA

PEREA

Luke's emphasis on
"Samaritan" stories,
Philip of Samaria's
influence
(Luke 9:51–56;10:25–37;
17:11–19 – all unique to
Luke!).

JUDEA

Jerusalem

Luke's, detailed knowledge of Mary's
story of Jesus' birth and childhood and
that of John the Baptist (Luke 1 and 2).
She was in Jerusalem with John; the
Apostle (John 19:25–27, Acts 1:14).

Luke highlights Christ's
Perean ministry
(Luke 9:56–18:34).

N
W — E
S

25. Recalling what you have learned in this study, try to reconstruct the outline below on the two areas of ministry in Caesarea:

   A. **Ministry of the "great" of this world**

      1) _____ , and his wife 2) _____

      3) _____

      4) _____ , and his sister 5) _____

   ✎ **Note:** Against your answers above, mark with "+" the only two of these who were Romans and with "x" the three who were half Jewish. For this you will have to look back to Frame 11 and the historical notes in Frames 13, 14 and 15.

   B. **Research work for the writing of**

      the Gospel according to _____ .

   ✎ **Note:** "A" above is certain.
      "B" is not certain, but a possibility based on considerable indirect evidence.

26. **To Think and Pray About**

   It must have been a traumatic experience for a man as active as Paul suddenly to have been faced with a prolonged period of captivity. It would have been all too easy for him to have slumped into depressed inactivity. As we have seen, this was far from the case, but rather it led to a vast new output on a most imaginative dimension!

   What can we learn from his example, when our plans are frustrated?

   What challenge does it hold out to Christians who are unemployed?

27. Now review and then do Test 6A.

Answers

25. A. 1)   + Felix
    2)   x Drusilla
    3)   + Festus
    4)   x Agrippa
    5)   x Bernice
    B. Luke

Lesson 6B

Journey to Rome

(Acts 27:1 to 28:15)

> *At last Paul was on his way to Rome, but not as he had planned. Instead he arrived as a prisoner to be tried before the Emperor Nero. What a prospect!*

The journey to Rome falls into four parts:

A.   The sea voyage to Crete.   Acts 27:1–12

B.   The storm and shipwreck.   Acts 27:13–44

C.   Three months in Malta.   Acts 28:1–10

D.   The last lap, to Rome.   Acts 28:11–16

Look at the map of the journey below.

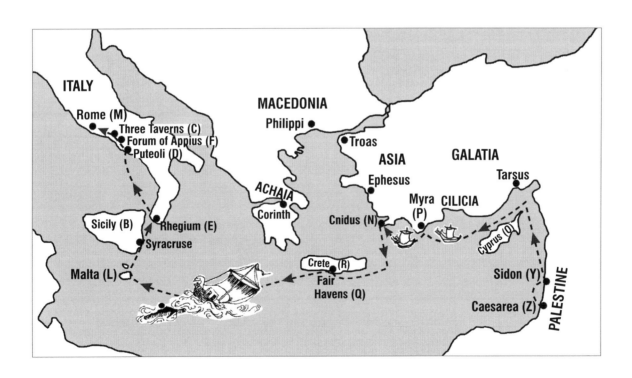

A. The Sea Voyage to Crete (Acts 27:1–12)

1. As a result of his appeal to be tried before Caesar, Paul was handed over to the care of a Roman officer called _____ (Acts 27:1), a most courteous man and one who was so obviously impressed by Paul, as we shall see, that one wonders if he became a Christian as a result of this historic journey with him!

2. From what Luke says in Acts 27:2 we can see that Paul was accompanied on this voyage by the Macedonian called a) _____ who was, you will remember, from the church in b) _____ (Acts 20:4). Further, from the pronouns used, we can tell that the author himself was also with them, that is c) _____, because it is one of the famous d) _____ passages. Draw a ring round "we" in Acts 27:2.

3. In Caesarea, letter a) _____ on the map on the Title Page of this lesson, they all boarded a ship that was westward bound. On arrival at b) _____ (v.3), marked on the map by the letter c) _____, Julius allowed Paul to go ashore to see his Christian friends who lovingly made sure that he had all that he d) _____ for the long journey (v.3).

4. Soon they were off the coast of the island to which Paul and Barnabas had gone on the first missionary journey, that is a) _____ (v.4) marked on the map by the letter b) _____. As they clung to the northern side of the island, to gain protection from the strong winds, they could make out the coastline of Cilicia, which once again would have brought back so many memories to Paul of his childhood days at Tarsus!

5. In Myra, marked on the map with the letter a) _____, they changed ships, this time to an African line bound for b) _____ (v.6). On her they continued to hug the mainland until the port of Cnidus in Asia, marked on the map by the letter c) _____, where instead of turning north toward Ephesus they tacked southwest and made for the island of d) _____ (v.7), marked on the map by the letter e) _____.

✎ **Note:** It was on this island that Titus later ministered, and he was here when Paul wrote his letter to him (Titus 1:5), as we shall see next week.

6. They made their way with difficulty to a port called a) _____ _____ (v.8), marked on the map by the letter b) _____, which by all accounts was not the kind of place in which to spend the c) _____ (v.12). So the captain and crew were all for attempting to reach a more agreeable town a little further down the coast. One man disagreed, and that was d) _____ (vv.9–10)! It was now well past "Yom Kippur" (which usually falls in our October), the Jewish _____ of _____ (also known as "the Fast") (v.9), and Paul knew that it would be f) _____ (v.10) to attempt a crossing, so he strongly advised them NOT to leave. Unhappily for all, he was overruled with the most terrible consequences, as we shall see. All this took place in Fair Havens on the island of Crete.

Answers

1. Julius	4. a) Cyprus
2. a) Aristarchus	b) O
b) Thessalonica	5. a) P
c) Luke	b) Italy
d) "we"	c) N
3. a) Z b) Sidon	d) Crete
c) Y d) needed	e) R
6. a) Fair Havens
b) Q
c) winter
d) Paul
e) Day/ Atonement
f) disastrous

B. The Storm and Shipwreck (Acts 27:13–44)

7. No sooner had they sailed than they were hit by a hurricane strength gale, called the a) "_____" (v.14). For days they were driven before the wind: things got so bad they began throwing some of the cargo overboard, but all to no avail. They could see neither b) _____ nor _____ (v.20) and so finally they gave up all hope of being saved. It was then that Paul stepped into the breach! He couldn't resist the temptation to say "I told you so! You should have taken my advice not to sail from c) _____" (v.21) he cried. But then he told them not to be afraid because God had sent his d) _____ (v.23–24) to tell him that although the ship would be lost not a man would perish!

8. They had now been a) _____ nights (v.27) in the storm when in the middle of the night a new danger threatened, this time from a plot among the b) _____ (v.30) to abandon ship in the lifeboat. Once again it was Paul who saved the situation by warning the c) _____ and the d) _____ (v.31) who cut the e) _____ (v.32) and let the boat go!

9. Paul was deeply concerned for the physical condition of all aboard because they had not eaten anything for a) _____ days (v.33). So just before dawn he urged them to have a good meal, saying that they would all be saved and that they would need all their strength in order to b) _____ (v.34). Then, suiting his action to his words, he took some c) _____ (v.35), publicly gave d) _____ to _____ before them all (v.35) and then ate. This courageous action put new life into everyone, and they all followed suit!

10. By now Paul had become the virtual captain of the ship! This amazing man of faith and action had so dominated the terrible situation that everybody was looking to him for a lead. Just then the ship hit a a) _____ (v.41): the front stuck fast, the back was smashed off by the force of the waves! As the b) _____ (v.42) prepared to kill all the c) _____, Julius suddenly intervened. It was contrary to all reason, because if any prisoner escaped Julius knew that he would have to pay for it with his own life. But during the voyage he had become so attracted to Paul that he wanted to save his life. So again, thanks to Paul, even the prisoners got safely to shore; some swimming, others clinging to broken bits of wreckage. The name of the island where they had been shipwrecked was d) _____ (Acts 28:1), marked on the map by the letter e) _____.

11. Now let's stop to think and pray. We can learn so much from the example of both **Paul** and **Luke** here. In each case, first read the words in the following box and then answer the questions by using this information.

Answers

7.	a) Northeaster	8.	d) soldiers	10.	a) sandbar	
	b) sun/ stars		e) ropes		b) soldiers	
	c) Crete	9.	a) 14		c) prisoners	
	d) angel		b) survive		d) Malta	
8.	a) 14		c) bread		e) L	
	b) sailors		d) thanks/ God			
	c) centurion					

A. Luke's Example

In the 19th century, a Scotsman named James Smith set out to reenact this historic voyage. Setting sail from Crete at exactly the same time of the year, he committed himself to the "northeaster" that had savaged Paul's ship, and guess what? In exactly fourteen days (compare Acts 27:27 and 33) he landed up on the same island of Malta! In other words, Luke's incredible accuracy as a historian has again been confirmed.

Now just consider: In the actual storm they had all given up hope of being saved (Acts 27:20). Apart from being overwhelmed by seasickness, Luke must have thought that all his notes would soon be buried at the bottom of the sea; so why continue writing his account? But he did continue because God had called him to this ministry, and so we have this accurate description today. What does this teach us about obedience and going on, even when humanly speaking there seems no point?

Luke's accuracy as an historian was wonderfully confirmed when a Scotsman called a) _____ _____ intentionally launched out from the island of b) _____ just at the time of the "northeaster". In c) _____ days, exactly the same time as Luke says, he landed up on the island of d) _____!

12.

B. Paul's Example

If any man had his heart in heaven with the Lord and yet his feet firmly set upon the ground, it was Paul. Just look at his faith and actions so far on this journey:

1. He alone had the common sense to see that it would be highly dangerous to leave port so late in the year.

2. And yet he was so closely in touch with God, in heaven, that it had been revealed to him that no one on the ship would perish.

3. It was Paul who had spotted the sailors' plot to abandon ship, and then, by prompt down-to-earth action, had foiled it.

4. It was Paul who was sufficiently practical to urge everybody to eat a good meal in preparation for the ordeal that awaited them in the raging waters.

5. And yet it was this same Paul who, without any embarrassment whatever, lifted his eyes to heaven to give God thanks for his food in front of all these hard-bitten soldiers and sailors.

Answers

11. a) James Smith
    b) Crete
    c) 14
    d) Malta

12. Continued.

How can you demonstrate from Paul's example that it is the man who is the most **heavenly minded** who is often also the **most earthly good**? Or at least, he should be! From the list of Paul's achievements above, write down the three you most appreciate, and then pray for help to be able to follow his example.

_____

_____

_____

_____

_____

C. Three Months in Malta (Acts 28:1–10)

13. The delightful account of their stay on the island of a) _____ (Acts 28:1) tells how the islanders showed them unusual b) _____ (v.2). Here again, Paul made a terrific impact on the islanders and no doubt on Julius and his Roman soldiers who also saw everything that was done. Luke describes in detail two miracles that God performed through Paul.

First: When Paul was helping to light a fire by gathering wood, a c) _____ (v.3) fastened itself to his hand. Paul merely shook it off into the fire and, to the astonishment of the islanders, was completely unharmed!

Second: The chief official of Malta was called d) _____ (v.7). When his father was taken seriously ill, Paul prayed for him and he was e) _____ (v.8).

Add these signs of God's blessing upon Paul to all that they had already observed in his life, and think of the effect they must have had upon Julius and the Roman guard!

D. The Last Lap, to Rome (Acts 28:11–16)

14. In all, they stayed on the island of Malta for a) _____ _____ (Acts 28:11) but at last it was time to say goodbye to their friends there as they embarked on a ship sailing for Italy. Their first port of call was Syracuse, on the large island of b) _____, marked on the map by the letter c) _____, where they stayed three days. From there it was a short hop over to the mainland of Southern Italy, at Rhegium, marked on the map by the letter d) _____. Then followed a pleasant two days' cruise up the west coast of Italy until they came to the port of e) _____ (v.13), marked on the map by the letter f) _____.

Answers

12. Any three from panel "B"	13. a) Malta	14. a) 3 months
	b) kindness	b) Sicily
	c) snake	c) B
	d) Publius	d) E
	e) healed	e) Puteoli
		f) D

15. Here they met some Christians who immediately invited them to stay in their home; and they stopped a whole a) _____ (v.14). Julius, the Roman commander, must have been impressed by this extraordinary show of hospitality (compare Romans 12:13). However, an even greater surprise awaited him! For when they reached the town called Forum of Appius, just over 40 miles out of Rome, marked on the map by the letter b) _____, a lovely crowd of Christians who had come all the way from Rome, were there to welcome and encourage Paul! Then, another 10 miles on, the same thing happened in the next town, called c) _____ _____ (v.15), marked on the map by the letter d) _____. Julius had never seen anything like it. What was it about this extraordinary Jew, Paul, that made people of all races, from a city that he had never visited before, come flocking to greet him with such joy and enthusiasm? Could it be that Christ was indeed the risen Son of God who united all these people, as Paul said?

16. And so they came to the great city of a) _____ (v.16), marked on the map by the letter b) _____. And so ended this most remarkable journey, and Paul's long standing hope to visit the capital of the Empire was finally fulfilled.

17. **To Think and Pray About**

    What were the two things that happened to Paul on the journey up the coast of Italy, that must have impressed his Roman guards so deeply?

    What does each of these things teach us about the ministry and witness of the church?

18. Now review and then do Test 6B.

Answers

15. a) week
    b) F
    c) Three Taverns
    d) C

16. a) Rome
    b) M

Lesson 6C

Paul: The Man of Joy

Letter to the Philippians

At last we have come to Paul's arrival in Rome! Luke, in Acts, gives us his usual pithy account of what happened, but we must turn to Paul's letters if we want to look beneath the surface. In this Group Study we will look again at Philippians, which Paul wrote from prison (probably his house arrest in Rome). It gives us a fantastic insight into his reactions during this terribly stressful situation.

1. How then did Paul, this very active man, react to being a prisoner? Was it with sorrowful resignation, and even depression, because he could no longer continue his missionary journeys? Read Philippians 2:17–18 which sets the tone for the whole letter. What message does it have for us?

   _____

   _____

   _____

Joy in Suffering

2. Just look how this **prison** letter is full of **joy**. The Greek words for **joy** and **rejoice** are used repeatedly by Paul throughout Philippians. Discuss the different things that Paul was able to "rejoice about" or "enjoy" while he was in prison, according to the following verses. Write **"joy"** in the margin of each verse.

   a) Philippians 1:4–5. _____

   _____

   _____

   b) Philippians 1:15–18. _____

   _____

   _____

   c) Philippians 1:18b–19. _____

   _____

   _____

    d)   Philippians 1:23–25. _____

_____

_____

    e)   Philippians 2:2. _____

_____

_____

    f)   Philippians 2:17–18. _____

_____

_____

_____

    g)   Philippians 4:1. _____

_____

_____

_____

    h)   Philippians 4:10. _____

_____

_____

3.   What a wonderful example Paul was of real JOY, even in suffering, both to the Philippian Christians and to us. So he was entitled to urge others to rejoice too.

From his own experience he was able to tell the Philippians what the secret of real joy was. What was it? (Phil. 3:1 and 4:4 – write **"joy"** in the margin by each of these verses.)

_____

_____

_____

4.   Paul hoped that the Philippians would draw strength from his example and the way he was able to suffer with **joy**, just as he in turn drew his strength from the example and Spirit of Jesus. Of course Jesus is the source of all our **joy** in suffering; but it is a wonderful encouragement and help to see this demonstrated with such total success in the life of others, namely Paul and the Philippians. Look at the following pictures.

a)   Which of the drawings show the suffering of each of the following:

- Christ?   _____

- Paul?   _____

- The kind of suffering the Philippian Christians could have endured?
  (Compare Philippians 1:29 and Luke 6:22–23)   _____

b)   How might you suffer for Christ's gospel today?
     How are Christians suffering in some other countries?

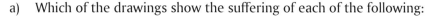

5.   Yes, Christ alone was the source of all their joy. Read Romans 8:17.

     What are the two things that every Christian is called upon to share with Christ if they are to experience something of real Christian joy?

6.   Now see how these are both illustrated in Philippians 2:5–11. Answer the following questions to get a general idea of this teaching.

     a)   What attitude must we have?

     b)   What nature did Christ **have**?

     c)   What nature did Jesus **take**?

     d)   What does this show us about his attitude to life?

e)   Where did God place Christ?

_____

f)   What did God give Jesus?

_____

g)   What posture will all take before Christ?

_____

h)   What will they all openly proclaim?

_____

7.   Some have described this as an early Christian hymn; that is why it is printed like a poem in the Bible. Say which verse or verses from the hymn corresponds to each of the pictures.

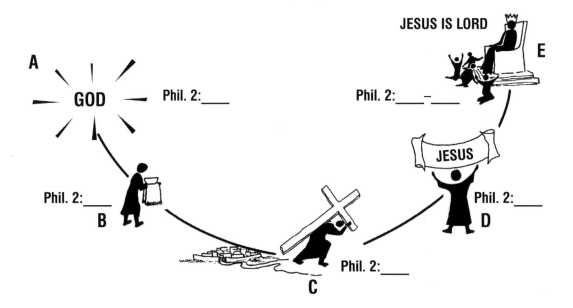

8.   We, too, are to share in Christ's suffering and ministry to this world. In what ways can we do this, according to Philippians 2:14–16?

_____

_____

_____

9.   Living in a world of corrupt and sinful people can often result in suffering, as in Paul's case. Sometimes his Roman citizenship helped him out. But what other citizenship did he (and do we) have, and what greater advantages does this bring us? Read Philippians 3:20–21.

_____

_____

10. Some Christians feel burdened by a sense of imperfection and this can easily rob them of their joy in Christ.

    What steps did Paul take to surmount this in his own situation according to Philippians 3:12–15a. and this picture, and how can this help us?

    _____

    _____

    _____

11. Read Jesus' words to his disciples, on the eve of his crucifixion, in John 16:20–22. Then compare this with Hebrews 12:2.

    How can fixing our eyes upon Jesus help us to experience something of his joy, even in times of sickness, disappointment, family difficulty, unemployment or opposition to our Christian witness?

    Do you have testimonies (either yours or of others)?

    _____

    _____

    _____

12. Jesus said:

    *"Ask and you will receive, that your **joy** (happiness) may be complete."* (John 16:24)

    Let's ask, that we may have the fullness of Christ's joy in our hearts, even as Paul did.

13. When you get home, please do

    a) Test 6C for this lesson.

    b) Lessons 7A and 7B in which we will learn more of Paul's ministry in Rome and also how he was released from prison for a further year or two, before finally being once again imprisoned and then martyred for his faith in Christ. Don't forget to do Test 7A and 7B.

    c) Lesson 7C.

Lesson 7A

Ministry in Rome

(Acts 28:16–31)

In a sense, Paul's ministry in Rome was just a natural continuation of that in Caesarea. This ministry was fourfold:
A.   Ministry to visitors
B.   Sending out envoys
C.   Writing
D.   Prayer
But first let's take a look at him settling into his new home in Rome.

Introduction: Arrival in Rome

1.   **Rome** was a city with more than a million freemen and a million slaves, that is, a population of over a) _____ _____ in all. It was by far the biggest city Paul had ever seen and he must have been so grateful to his Christian friends who had hired a house in readiness for him and could orientate him in this strange metropolis. So Paul was in his own b) _____ house (Acts 28:30), but in chains and guarded all the time by a succession of Roman c) _____ (v.16). However, he was happy because he had a stream of visitors who were all made d) _____ (v.30) and to whom he preached about the e) _____ of _____ (v.31) and taught about the Lord Jesus Christ. This he did for a period of f) _____ years (v.30), easy to remember because it was the same time as he had spent as a prisoner in g) _____ (Acts 24:1, 27).

2.   It must have been a wonderful home to visit. The regular members of the household were the two who had accompanied him on his hazardous journey from Caesarea: these were his dear doctor friend a) _____ (Col. 4:14) and his young convert from Thessalonica, b) _____ (Col. 4:10). Then there was the founder of the church in Colossae, c) _____ (Col. 4:12) and, until he was sent on a journey as Paul's envoy, there was his beloved son in the faith d) _____ (Col. 1:1). What a group it must have been! Judging from Paul's remarks in Ephesians 5:19, the house must have been filled from morning to evening with the sound of e) _____.

Answers

1.   a) two million
     b) rented
     c) soldiers
     d) welcome
     e) kingdom/ God
     f) 2
     g) Caesarea

2.   a) Luke
     b) Aristarchus
     c) Epaphras
     d) Timothy
     e) singing

3. Paul didn't waste any time! After this terrific journey (plus being shipwrecked) he allowed himself just a) _____ days (Acts 28:17) to recuperate and get his new house in order before he called the local b) _____ leaders (v.17) to a meeting! Remember that there was a huge Jewish community in Rome, so Paul fixed a date to invite them all to his house: a c) _____ number (v.23) came and listened to Paul from morning to night. As usual there was a divided response, some were d) _____ (v.24), others would not e) _____ (v.24). So this leads us to the first aspect of Paul's ministry:

A. Ministry to Visitors

4. We have already seen the first visitors Paul had in his home. As he had already written to the Romans, it was his unbroken custom to preach first to the a) _____ (Rom. 1:16). As many of the Jews would not believe, Paul then turned to the b) _____ (Acts 28:28) who he was sure would c) _____.

5. One day Paul was both surprised and delighted to receive a visit from Barnabas' cousin, _____ (Col. 4:10). Paul had obviously forgiven Mark for deserting him on the first missionary journey twelve years before, and was able to commend him warmly to the church in Colossae where apparently he hoped to visit. This event must have brightened Paul's day, and healed a deep wound in his heart.

6. On another occasion he was visited by a runaway slave from Colossae named a) _____ (Phm. v.10) who had fled the household of none other than the leader of the Colossian church, called b) _____ (Phm. vv.1 and 2). With infinite tact and understanding Paul had been able to win this slave for Christ and in this letter calls him "*my* c) _____" (v.10).

7. According to the barbarous customs of those days, Philemon had a perfect right to kill his slave Onesimus for running away, but Paul now asked Onesimus to return to his home in Colossae and present himself to Philemon, asking his **Christian forgiveness**. At the same time he sent a most moving letter to Philemon (one of the gems of literature), asking him to forgive Onesimus, and another letter to the whole church in Colossae calling upon them to be tolerant one of another and to a) _____ one another (Col. 3:13). Of course Paul was taking a huge risk. Humanly speaking he was expecting (and praying for) a miracle as big as that of raising a dead person to life, but in the more fragile area of human relationships. Apparently the miracle took place and Philemon must have received Onesimus back, now no more as his b) _____ but as a dear c) _____ in Christ (Phm. v.16).

Answers

3. a) 3	4. a) Jews	7. a) forgive
b) Jewish	b) Gentiles	b) slave
c) large	c) listen	c) brother
d) convinced	5. Mark	
e) believe	6. a) Onesimus	
	b) Philemon	
	c) son	

8. **To Think and Pray About**

    Jesus taught us to pray, *"Forgive us our sins as we forgive everyone who sins against us"*. From Paul's experiences with his two visitors above, John Mark and Onesimus, how can we see that he was willing to put into practice in his own relationships what he was always asking others to do in theirs? Read again Colossians 3:13 prayerfully, asking for a **real** change in your attitudes and relationships, in accord with this teaching, with that person you find particularly difficult.

9. Another very welcome visitor who had brought gifts from the church in Philippi was a) _____ (Phil. 4:18). He had also set to and helped Paul in countless ways. Then suddenly he had been taken seriously b) _____ and had nearly c) _____ (Phil. 2:27). However God spared his life and so Paul sent him back to his home church.

10. Perhaps the most far-reaching effects of this ministry were to those who were his **involuntary** visitors, the succession of a) _____ (Acts 28:16) who guarded him day and night. Paul was keenly interested in all their affairs as we can see from his vivid description of their equipment, which he uses as an illustration of the Christian's b) _____ (Eph. 6:11–18). It was a golden opportunity to spread the gospel among those who would travel far and wide throughout the Empire! When Paul says that the whole palace c) _____ (Phil. 1:13) knew he was a Christian, and then sends greetings from those from d) _____ household (Phil. 4:22) surely it indicates that some of these must have been soldiers who had been converted in this way.

11. As with us all, Paul also had his failures. In both Colossians 4:14 and Philemon, verse 24, Paul mentions a) D_____. In the last letter that he wrote, Paul sadly tells Timothy that when things got too hot for this man he had b) _____ Paul (2 Tim. 4:10) because of his obsession with this present c) _____ .

    B. Sending out Envoys

12. There was not only a stream of people coming **into** Paul's home but also a stream of **envoys** going out from it, through whom he kept in touch with all the churches. For example, the bearer of his two letters to Colossae, one to the church and the other to Philemon, was a) _____ (Col. 4:7) who had been one of the representatives from b) _____ (Acts 20:4) in Paul's band of delegates that carried his Aid Fund to Jerusalem. From another of Paul's letters we can see that he was also Paul's envoy to the church in c) _____ (Eph. 6:21).

Commissioning

    Remember that this envoy was sent to two of the churches in Asia, namely d) _____ and e) _____ . With him went Philemon's runaway slave, f) _____ (Col. 4:9).

Answers

9. a) Epaphroditus	11. a) Demas	12. d) Ephesus
b) ill	b) deserted	e) Colossae
c) died	c) world	f) Onesimus
10. a) soldiers	12. a) Tychicus	
b) armor	b) Asia	
c) guard	c) Ephesus	
d) Caesar's		

13. From another of Paul's letters that he wrote at this time, we can see that he hoped to send his dear colleague a) _____ (Phil. 2:19) as his envoy to the church in b) _____ in the province of c) _____.

14. **Review**

    Paul's envoy to Colossae and Ephesus was a) _____.

    Paul's envoy to Philippi was b) _____.

C. Writing

15. We have already seen that during his period of house arrest in Rome Paul wrote four of his loveliest letters. Look at Supplement 1 where you will find these listed. They are:

    Writing

    a) _____   b) _____

    c) _____   d) _____

    Then you should remember that Paul also wrote another letter to Asia, which is not included in the New Testament because it has since been lost; this is the letter to e) _____ (Col. 4:16).

16. Read carefully the following verses which have something in common as regards the condition in which Paul found himself at the time of writing each of these four New Testament letters. Ephesians 3:1; Colossians 4:3; Philippians 1:7; Philemon, verse 23.

    The thing that is common to all these letters is that Paul was writing them from a) _____. For this and other reasons the traditional belief has been that he wrote them during this period of house arrest in b) _____.

    Note: There are other theories, but we prefer to keep to the traditional one which is the most probable.

17. Also, it is almost certain that this was the time when the third Gospel was completed by a) _____, who in turn may have been ably assisted by b) _____! Certainly all the circumstances as we know them point to this. In his letters to Colossae and to Philemon Paul tells how c) L_____ was with him (Col. 4:14 and Phm. v.24).

    Perhaps equally significant is the fact that in the very same breath he says that the writer of the **second** Gospel was **also** with them, that is d) _____! (Phm. v.24 and Col. 4:10. Look also at 2 Tim. 4:11.) Mark (tradition suggests) seems to have written his Gospel from the things he had heard Peter preach about and we can't be sure whether it was already written or not. Either way, wouldn't **Luke and Mark** have spent hours together in Paul's house comparing

Answers

13. a) Timothy	15. a) Ephesians	16. a) prison
b) Philippi	b) Colossians	b) Rome
c) Macedonia	c) Philemon	17. a) Luke
14. a) Tychicus	d) Philippians	b) Paul
b) Timothy	e) Laodicea	c) Luke
		d) Mark

notes? It certainly would seem probable. And if this were the case, can you imagine Paul sitting around inactive without giving a spot of advice to both of them?

18. **To Think and Pray About**

On the first missionary journey Mark's deserting led to an unhappy split between Paul and Barnabas (Acts 15:36–40). Yet had Mark continued in Paul's team his Gospel would probably merely have echoed Luke's. The break with Paul led to a new relationship with Peter from whom Mark got fresh material. The split was wrong but God overruled it to give us two Gospels with fascinatingly different, yet complementary, pictures of Christ. How does this illustrate what Paul says in Romans 8:28 and what experience do you have of this truth?

19. **Review**

Although we can never be certain of the details, it seems safe to say that this period of house arrest in Rome was when Paul and his team were engaged, among all the other things, in a most fruitful ministry of writing. The **four** most certain letters written are:

a) _____

b) _____

c) _____

d) _____

We also suggest that it is highly probable that Paul played his part in writing the third Gospel, which is the one according to e) _____. Finally, on finishing the Gospel, Luke (with Paul's help) would have gone right on with the writing of his second book, f) "The _____ of the _____". What a productive period it was.

20. We have seen three of the four principal aspects of Paul's ministry in Rome. We must now add and examine the fourth which was the foundation of all the others:

1) M_____ to V_____

2) S_____ out E_____

3) W_____

4) P_____ (Eph. 3:14)

Answers

19. a) Ephesians
    b) Philippians
    c) Colossians
    d) Philemon
    e) Luke
    f) Acts/ Apostles

20. 1) Ministry to Visitors
    2) Sending out Envoys
    3) Writing
    4) Prayer

D. Prayer

Prayer

21. Paul would have been the first to say that all the other aspects of his ministry depended **entirely** on this fourth one — **prayer**. Fortunately we have the exact text of several of Paul's wonderful prayers in his letters. The references of these are given below.

    Read these now, and try and build up a mental picture of Paul at prayer. What are the requests that fill his prayers? Now compare with your own. How could you improve?

    According to the custom of those days, Paul would have prayed and read *aloud*, so try and picture to yourself the effect that this would have had on the succession of Roman soldiers who were constantly guarding him.

    How Paul Prayed:
    - Ephesians 1:15–20 and 3:14–21
    - Philippians 1:4–5 and 1:9–11
    - Colossians 1:9–10
    - Philemon, verses 4 and 6

    How Paul Praised:
    - Ephesians 5:19–20
    - Colossians 3:16

22. **To Think About**

    Paul was in chains! But Paul knew that there was something that they could never chain up! What was this? (2 Tim. 2:9).

    Think of ways in which, far from binding God's word, Paul made it run everywhere.

    What does this teach us about our total victory over even the worst of **circumstances**, if we are in Christ. To what extent are you enjoying your victory? How could you improve?

23. Now review and then do Test 7A.

Lesson 7B

Between Imprisonments: Then the Glory

(1 and 2 Timothy, and Titus)

1. Luke ends his account in the Acts very **abruptly** with Paul still a prisoner under house arrest in Rome. But from Paul's remaining letters it seems fairly certain that he was released for a period of about four years before finally being arrested again. Indeed, the letters of his *first* imprisonment show that he was hoping to be released soon because he asks Philemon to get a a) _____ _____ ready for him in Colossae (Phm. v.22). In Philippians 1:19 he tells them that he is pretty sure that he will be released thanks to their b) _____ and the _____ given by the Spirit of Christ.

2. Look at Supplement 1 in order to answer the following questions:

   It appears that Paul was imprisoned in Rome on a) _____ occasions. Between these imprisonments he probably had a further period of freedom of about b) _____ years' duration. During this free period he revisited many of his churches and wrote c) _____ more letters, one to d) _____ who was by then in e) _____ (1 Tim. 1:3), and the other to f) _____ who was looking after the churches in g) _____ (Titus 1:5). Then he was arrested again, probably in the year h) _____ A.D. In this final imprisonment he wrote his last letter, which was i) ____ _____, just before he was killed for his faith in Christ. Our next Group Study will be on this last letter. But first let's consider...

   ### A. The Period between His Imprisonments

3. Although we cannot tell the exact order in which things happened in the period between his imprisonments we **can** trace a number of the places Paul visited (many of which are already familiar to us). For example, during his **final** imprisonment he writes (2 Tim. 4:20) that he had left Erastus in a) _____, marked on this map by the letter b) _____ and Trophimus in c) _____, letter d) _____. Then he also speaks of having left some of his scanty belongings in e) _____ (2 Tim. 4:13), letter f) _____; and he asks Timothy to pick them up some time and bring them to him in Rome.

Answers

1. a) guest room	2. d) Timothy	3. a) Corinth
b) prayers/ help	e) Ephesus	b) D
2. a) 2	f) Titus	c) Miletus
b) 4	g) Crete	d) A
c) 2	h) 67	e) Troas
	i) 2 Timothy	f) C

From his words in 1 Timothy 1:3 it seems that at one time he must also have left Timothy in g) _____, letter h) _____, on his way to i) _____. Finally, in Titus 3:12 he asks Titus, from Crete, letter j) _____, to meet him next winter in k) _____, letter l) _____. So already some kind of pattern of his movements is emerging. We can see that in spite of his misgivings that he would never see them again, stated to the Ephesian elders when he said goodbye at the end of his third journey, he did indeed visit them once more, as well as returning to the churches in the provinces of Macedonia and Achaia.

4. Apart from these references in Paul's letters, there is also an interesting bit of evidence from history about Paul's movements at this time. Read Panel "A" before answering the questions below.

> **PANEL "A"**
>
> You will remember how on his third missionary journey Paul was talking about going on from Rome to the country of **Spain** (Rom. 15:24). His fateful visit to Jerusalem had prevented this at the time. However, writing only 30 years later, Clement of Rome said that Paul "reached the farthest bounds of the West". Could this mean that Paul did reach Spain in these years between his imprisonments? We shall never know for certain, but it is possible. Once Paul had got an idea into his head he didn't easily let it go!

"Paul reached the farthest bounds of the a) _____": so wrote b) _____ only c) _____ years after Paul's final imprisonment. This phrase written by someone in d) _____ most probably would have been referring to the country of e) _____ as a quick look at the map in Lesson 4A.4 will show. We know that Paul wanted to visit there, and so it is quite possible that he achieved his ambition during this period of f) _____ years between his imprisonments, although we can never be absolutely sure of this.

B. Letters Written in Period between Imprisonments

5. **Review**

Between his imprisonments Paul wrote a) ____ _____ and b) _____. During his last imprisonment he wrote c) ____ _____, just before his d) _____. This last letter we will consider in our next and final Group Study. For the moment we will look very briefly at the other two, and the people to whom they were written.

6. **Titus** was one of Paul's earliest associates. Indeed he had gone with Paul to Jerusalem on that historic occasion when some of the Jewish Christians had tried to get Titus a) _____ (Gal. 2:3–4). As he was a pure Gentile, Paul had prevented this.

Answers

3. g) Ephesus
   h) B
   i) Macedonia
   j) F
   k) Nicopolis
   l) E

4. a) West
   b) Clement
   c) 30
   d) Rome
   e) Spain
   f) 4

5. a) 1 Timothy
   b) Titus
   c) 2 Timothy
   d) death

6. a) circumcised

On the third missionary journey, he had also been Paul's valued envoy to the church in b) _____ (2 Cor. 7:6–7) and was in large measure responsible for the healing of a really dreadful situation there. Now we find him responsible for the new churches on the island of c) _____ .

7. **Timothy** was, of course, Paul's a) _____ in the faith. He had led him to faith in Christ on the first missionary journey to Galatia. In his second letter to him Paul recalls those far-off days when he had visited the Galatian towns of b) _____, c) _____ and d) _____ (2 Tim. 3:11). Now we find him responsible for the church in e) _____ .

8. It is interesting to note how similar these two letters are in both style and content, which is only to be expected as they were both written about the same time to two of Paul's colleagues who were seeking to pastor churches. Compare briefly 1 Timothy 3:1–7 with Titus 1:5–9; you can see that both of these passages have instructions on the kind of l_____ that were to be appointed in the churches. This is why these letters are often called the "pastoral" letters.

Note: We have studied 1 and 2 Timothy in considerable detail in Lesson 2 in Book 2, when we looked at Paul's methods of training Timothy. If you have this, look back to it now to refresh your memory. These four years of renewed freedom must have slipped away all too quickly, and soon ended tragically in...

C. Paul's Second Imprisonment

9. Now read Panel "B" before answering the following questions.

> **PANEL "B"**
>
> These were dark years indeed for the Christians. The Emperor Claudius had by now been replaced by the infamous NERO who in the year 64 A.D. was responsible for the fearful massacre of the Christians whom he blamed falsely for the burning of Rome. Some were flung to the lions, others tarred all over and then lifted up on crosses and lighted as living torches, to be paraded around the streets at night. The Christians went underground; literally, for they hid in the warren of tombs (catacombs) that crisscrossed under the outskirts of Rome. It seems that, with many others, Paul was again seized and thrown into prison, this time not under house arrest but into the fearful dungeons that awaited many of those who would not deny the name of Christ. His aged body must have been racked by pain as he spent the long, cold nights on the stone slab floors. It was damp, and stinking from almost nonexistent sanitation.

Answers

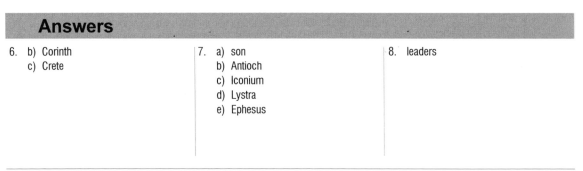

6. b) Corinth
   c) Crete

7. a) son
   b) Antioch
   c) Iconium
   d) Lystra
   e) Ephesus

8. leaders

How different was Paul's situation in prison now to that of his first imprisonment. Then he had been under a) _____ arrest; now he was in a horrible and insanitary b) _____. The Emperor, named c) _____, was conducting one of the worst persecutions that the Christians had ever had to suffer, so many of them went underground and hid in the d) _____ beneath the outskirts of e) _____.

10. Under these circumstances many Christians just couldn't face up to such stress, and so Paul sadly has to say that many in Asia had a) _____ him (2 Tim. 1:15). They had apparently fled, much as the apostles had when Jesus had been taken prisoner. Even worse, at his first trial b) ____ _____ (2 Tim. 4:16) stood by him. Yet even so it is clear that at this trial before Nero, Paul succeeded in turning his witness box into a pulpit! He was able, he says, to proclaim the full c) _____ (2 Tim. 4:17) for all the Gentiles to hear. The sense of loneliness must have been dreadful; yet Paul was still wonderfully aware of one who stood with him, that was the d) _____ (2 Tim. 4:17). Miraculously on this occasion he was rescued from being sentenced to e) _____ (2 Tim. 4:17). It was in this situation that, just before a further trial in which he was condemned to death by the fiendish Nero, Paul wrote one of his loveliest letters, 2 Timothy (which we will look at in our next and final Group Study).

D. Paul's Martyrdom

11. The circumstances of Paul's death are not told in the Bible, however, writings from the Church Fathers (Clement, Tertullian, Eusebius and others) indicate that, as a Roman citizen, he was beheaded with a military sword, during the severe persecution under Nero around the year 67 A.D. He was completely unafraid as he faced death, even exuberant at the prospect of at last being with Christ. We can tell this from the things he wrote:

"I desire to depart and be with Christ, which is a) _____ by _____." (Philippians 1:23)

"I have finished the race, I have kept the faith. Now there is in store for me the b) _____ of righteousness." (2 Timothy 4:7–8)

"Who shall separate us from the c) _____ of Christ? Shall trouble... or danger or sword?" (Romans 8:35)

"I consider that our present d) _____ are not worth comparing with the glory..." (Romans 8:18)

Answers

9. a) house
   b) dungeon
   c) Nero
   d) tombs or catacombs
   e) Rome

10. a) deserted
    b) no one
    c) message
    d) Lord
    e) death

11. a) better by far
    b) crown
    c) love
    d) sufferings

So as the soldiers escorted Paul out of the gates of Rome, hardly a head turned to observe the plight of one of the greatest men who had ever lived. A death squad was pretty tame stuff in Nero's Rome, drunk with the sadistic spectacles of gladiatorial butchery and of defenseless people being torn to bits by the wild beasts. So who cared what happened to this unattractive little Jew, being hustled to his cruel death? But God did. He looked a little deeper, and awaited him with open arms, and Paul knew it!

12.   Now review and then do Test 7B.

Lesson 7C

Paul the Aged: Still Looking Forward
2 Timothy Written

After about 30 years of serving Christ Paul prepares to leave this life. In his second letter to Timothy we have the last recorded words of the great apostle. Here Paul speaks to us across the centuries as he awaits execution. He tells us of some of the important things he wants remembered by those who will carry on the ministry of Christ. Let's listen carefully to what he says. We will look at three aspects of Paul's forward look.

Paul looking forward:

A. **to his own future in glory with Christ.**

B. **to Timothy's future as he carried on the work.**

C. **to the Church in our day and age, "the last days".**

A. Looking Forward: to His Own Future in Glory with Christ

1. Read what Paul wrote in 2 Timothy 4:6–8 during his second imprisonment and then compare it with the statement in Philippians 3:12–14 from his first imprisonment that we studied last week.

    a) What theme is common to these statements?

    _____

    b) What is the main difference, and what do you think caused this?

    _____

    _____

✎ **Note:** Write "the prize" in the margin of both these passages.

2. If we were facing the end of our life and work how would we feel?

    _____

    _____

    _____

    _____

    _____

    _____

3. So let's see if Paul has something to tell us in 2 Timothy 4:8.

    a) How do we know that Paul isn't only speaking about his own **personal** expectations here but is also expressing what should be the attitude of all Christians when facing death?

        _____

    b) What should this Christian attitude to death be?

        _____

4. How can a person approaching the end, who perhaps is suffering as Paul was, be **sure** that their future is **secure**?

    Read 2 Timothy 1:9, 11–12 and then compare with what Jesus said in John 14:2–3.

    _____

    _____

    _____

5. On approaching the end of life there are often **two** main concerns that preoccupy people:

    •   concern for themselves, and what awaits them in the valley of death and after.

    •   concern for their loved ones that they have to leave behind.

    Which of these

    a) most preoccupies you?

        _____

        _____

        _____

    b) most preoccupied Paul? Phil. 1:21–26. Write "prize" in the margin.

        _____

        _____

        _____

    So let's see the second thing that Paul looked forward to as he faced death...

B. Looking Forward: to Timothy's Future as He Carried On the Work

6. Paul was certainly no starry-eyed wishful thinker waiting for the golden age to dawn automatically. Of all men, Paul was a realist and saw only too clearly all the agony through which the church would have to pass. We see this from his warnings to Timothy about the future conditions in which the gospel must be preached. So Paul's concern about his near execution was not at all for himself, but for the welfare of the churches he would be leaving behind. Read 2 Timothy 3:1–5.

What could Paul see would be the attitude of many in the future to

a)   themselves?

_____

_____

b)   others?

_____

_____

c)   God?

_____

_____

7.   How many of these things will our children and loved ones have to face? What other clouds hang over them?

_____

_____

_____

8.   Paul realized that it would be against this kind of background that Christians would have to preach and spread the gospel as he himself had done. So although he is confident that God is going to keep them, he nevertheless does everything in his power to prepare Timothy and the church to stand firm through it all.

Faced with such a prospect what was to be Timothy's (and our) sure defense?
Read 2 Timothy 3:13–17.

_____

_____

9.   Paul saw only too clearly that the Christian message would have to be lived and spread amidst people who would be totally self-centered, materialistic and even whose religion would be a sham. But this only made him redouble his efforts to prepare the church to surmount these dangers. What further practical advice did he give to Timothy in these circumstances (and to us)? Read 2 Timothy 4:3–5.

_____

_____

_____

_____

But Paul, now an old man, sees even further into the future...

C. Looking Forward: to the Church in Our Day and Age, "the Last Days"

10. Paul does not only have Timothy in mind; his great mind stabs through the centuries as he concerns himself with the whole future of the church even down to us today!

    a) What phrase in 2 Timothy 3:1 tells us this?

    _____

    b) What provision did Paul make for the long-term future of the church in 2 Timothy 2:2?

    _____

    _____

    c) We have come to the end of a very demanding course of Bible study. God forbid that it will prove to be no more than a mere mental exercise. Can you think of practical steps to take now that would ensure that you can pass on to others what we have learned?

    _____

    _____

    _____

11. So Paul, now an old man and facing death, was still **looking forward** with great confidence, in spite of every kind of difficulty. Read the passage under the picture.

"I press on toward the goal to win the prize." (Phil. 3:14)

As regards his own future, he was certainly looking forward keenly to seeing his beloved Lord and Master face to face. And as regards the church of God, Paul's massive faith spanned the ages, piercing the darkest gloom, as he saw, stretching out over the centuries, a succession of faithful men who in turn would pass the gospel message on to others, right down to the last day when Christ would return again. Just look how amazingly his hopes have been realized! And we are in that same glorious succession of passing on the truth... may we honor the Lord, by following Paul's great example of faith and service. I hope you have been helped in this by having pondered together the life of one who could say with total honesty:

"For to me, to live is Christ and to die is gain." (Phil. 1:21)

Let's pray together that we, as his successors, will not betray this confidence.

12. a) We only have two **Review** lessons for next week, before the final exam. Please follow the instructions at the top of Lesson 8 with great care.

    ✎ **Note:** These lessons will also serve you in good stead as an Index in future days if you want to look up any special point.

    b) If you have time, review all the **Tests**; it is one of the best ways to review the course objectives.

    c) Finally go over the pictures as they often highlight main points; also all the places marked on the Test Map.

Lesson 8A
Index: Paul's Life – Review

1. First try and answer aloud to yourself the questions in a particular number from what you can remember from your lessons.

2. Whenever you are not sure of an answer look it up in the part of the lesson given in the reference and review it well.

3. This review of Paul's life, Lesson 8A, falls into **three** parts. Try and do one of these parts thoroughly for each of the first three days and then Lesson 8B, review of Paul's letters and general review for the rest of the week:

   Part 1 – Ephesus.

   Part 2 – Macedonia and Achaia revisited.

   Part 3 – A prisoner in Caesarea, Crete, Malta and Rome.

4. The Review Lessons 8A and 8B can also serve as an **index** in future days, if you want to look up any information about Paul's life and letters.

Part 1: Ephesus

1. **Paul Approaches Ephesus Via Galatia (1A.6)**

   On each of Paul's missionary journeys he always visited the churches he had established on his previous journeys. On his third journey, therefore, he passed through Galatia on his way to Asia.

   a) What special help did they give to Paul on this visit?

   b) In which verse in 1 Corinthians 16 does Paul mention this?

   c) What was the name of Paul's faithful companion who originally came from the churches in Galatia? Which town did he come from?

2. **A New Teacher from Africa in Ephesus (1A.7 to 11)**

   While Paul was still traveling through Galatia a new teacher from Africa arrived in Ephesus. What was

   a) his name?

   b) nationality?

   c) the city and continent of his birth?

   d) the only baptism that he knew?

   e) the two people who instructed him more fully in the truth?

   f) the city to which he now went, supported by a letter of recommendation from the brethren in Ephesus?

   g) the unhappy result of his visit there?

3. Paul's Early Days in Ephesus (Pictures A, B, and C in 1B.1)

At last Paul arrived in **Ephesus**! Some of his earliest contacts were a group of new Christians.

a) How many of them were there? (1B.8)

b) What was the only baptism they knew? (1B.8)

c) In whose name did Paul baptize them? (1B.9)

d) What did they receive as a result? (1B.9)

e) How was this demonstrated on this occasion? (1B.9)

f) What were the **three** illustrations that Paul used in his letter to Ephesus, some years later, to explain more fully what this signified in their lives? (Pictures in 1C.9, 10 and 11.)

g) How did Paul earn his living while he was in Ephesus? (1B.6)

h) How did Paul use much of the money that he earned? (1B.5)

4. Preaching and Teaching in Ephesus (Picture B in 1B.1)

As was his custom, Paul first went and preached in the Jewish synagogue in Ephesus. Soon he was forced to leave through the opposition of the unbelieving Jews. So he moved to a public place.

a) Where did he now preach? (2A.2)

b) How long was he there? (2A.2)

c) Apart from this public place, where else did he teach? (1B.7)

5. Ministry to the Whole of Asia)

Although apparently Paul himself stayed in Ephesus, nevertheless his message spread throughout the whole of Asia. (Try and build up a picture in your mind of what happened at this time by reviewing 2A.5 to 11, especially the picture in 11. Also 7A.6 and 7.)

a) What were the three ways in which the gospel spread throughout Asia? (2A.10)

b) What was the name of the rich slave owner who was converted on a visit to Ephesus at this time? (2A.9)

c) What was the name of his runaway slave? (7A.6)

d) Why did this slave later return to his master? (7A.7)

e) What was their home town, situated in the Lycus valley? (2C.2)

f) Where did the church meet in this town? (2A.6)

g) What was the name of the evangelist who set up this church? (2A.6)

h) Paul wrote **two** letters to this town, one personal, the other to the whole church. What are these letters called? (2A.10)

i) What were the main problems that Paul tried to answer in the first of these letters, that to the church in general? And what answers did Paul give? (2C.6 and 8)

j) What other two churches did he set up nearby? (2A.5)

k) To which of these did Paul also write a letter, which is now lost? (2A.10)

6. Ministry to Corinth from Ephesus (Picture B in 2B.4 and Supplement 2)

Unfortunately at this time really big trouble was brewing up in Corinth.

a) Initially this trouble seems to have been associated with the visit that Apollos had made there. What was this trouble? (2B.8 and 9)

b) In the New Testament we only have two of the letters that Paul wrote to Corinth. However from these we can see that he must have written other letters to them that have since been lost. How many letters did he write to Corinth in all? What are the lost letters usually called? (2B.14; 3A.4 and 3B.11)

c) In which verse in 1 Corinthians 16 does Paul tell us that he was in Ephesus at the time of writing this letter? (2B.12)

d) What were the main problems that Paul tried to answer in 1 Corinthians? (2B.19 to 29)

e) How many of the **four** letters to Corinth were written from Ephesus? (Suppl. 2)

f) How many were written from Macedonia (probably Philippi)? Which? (Suppl. 2)

g) Also he must have made a quick visit to Corinth from Ephesus (which is not told in the Acts but is mentioned in 2 Corinthians). What is this journey usually called? (3B.15)

h) Who visited Corinth on Paul's behalf after that visit? (3B.8)

i) What was one of his principal tasks there, apart from trying to bring peace into the church again? (3B.8)

7. Paul's Future Plans from Ephesus (2B.2 and 3)

It was in Ephesus that we see that Paul first began planning to go to **Rome**.

a) Find the passage in Acts that tells us this.

b) To which places did he intend to go first?

c) Whom did he send ahead of him to Macedonia?

8. Clashes With Unbelievers in Ephesus (Pictures in 2A.12; Pictures A to F in 3A.7)

From the Acts we know that Paul had **two** major confrontations with unbelievers in Ephesus.

a) The first was with the seven sons of a Jew. What was his name? And what did they try and do unsuccessfully? What happened as a result? (2A.13 to 16)

b) The second confrontation was with a silversmith. What was his name? Why was he so against Paul? What did he do as a result? (3A.8 to 18)

c) What good took place in the church as a result of the first of these confrontations? (2A.17 and 18)

9. Anguish in Ephesus (Picture A in 2B.4)

We can see from the Acts that Paul passed through a period of great tribulation during his final months in Ephesus. From his letters we can see that it was even worse. He passed through such anguish that he actually despaired of life.

a) To what did he liken this experience in 1 Corinthians? Find the reference. (2B.5 and 6)

b) But it is in 2 Corinthians that he truly lays bare his heart on the matter. What two wonderful illustrations did Paul use in this letter to show how, in Christ, God's strength is manifested in our weakness? (3C.3, 6 and 9).

10. Paul Leaves Ephesus (Pictures in 3A.7 and 17)

a) Where was Titus when Paul left Ephesus? (3A.16)

b) Where did Paul wait for Titus? (3A.16)

c) Why was he so desperate to see Titus again? (3A.16)

d) Did Titus meet Paul in this town, as Paul had hoped? If not, where? (3B.9)

Now review Part 1, before going on.

Part 2: Macedonia and Achaia Revisited

11. Outreach from Macedonia and Philippi (Picture in 3B.1)

a) This return to Philippi was notable for two more of Paul's tremendous achievements. Which were these? (3B.6)

b) Here Paul met up once again with Luke. Who else arrived at this time (from Corinth)? (3B.3)

c) Was the news he brought good or bad? (3B.6)

d) Where did Paul ask him to go now? (3B.6)

e) Which of his letters did he send with him? (3B.6)

f) What was the central message of this wonderful letter (3B.11))?

g) In which two chapters of this letter does Paul deal in detail with his proposed visit to Jerusalem? (3B.11)

h) From here Paul began a whole new evangelistic thrust. Into which new province did he go with the gospel? (3B.4)

12. Eventful Three Months in Corinth (Lesson 4A)

Thanks to the ministry of Titus and of Paul's letters, the Christians in Corinth had at last settled down in peace.

a) Which of his letters did Paul now write? (4A.7)

b) In whose house was he writing? (4A.8)

c) What great new evangelistic venture was Paul now planning? (4A.3 to 5)
Find the passage in the letter he was writing, where Paul speaks of this.

d) Which church did he hope would be a base for this new venture? (4A.5)

e) The **theme** of this letter were very similar to Galatians. Why was the **style** of the letter so different? (4A.11 and 12)

f) What was the main theme of this letter? (4A.9 and 10)

g) What two groups of people did Paul especially have in mind throughout this letter? Think of examples to show this. (4A.13; 4B.8 and 5C)

h) In which chapter of this letter did Paul describe the terrible sins of the people in Corinth? (4B.3)

13. Journey Back to Jerusalem Via Macedonia, Troas and Miletus

Paul had intended journeying directly from Corinth to Jerusalem; however he was prevented in this. (5A.1 to 7)

a) What prevented him? (5A.2)

b) Where did he go instead? (5A.2)

c) He was accompanied by quite a large group; what was their function? (5A.3)

d) It was now that Luke once again started to travel with Paul. How do we know this? About how many years had it been since they had last traveled together? (3B.3)

What was the first town that they visited after leaving Philippi on the return journey to Jerusalem? (5A.7)

e) What miracle did Paul do there? (Picture "C" in 5A.9)

f) Then they traveled south toward Ephesus again (see map in 5A.10), but they sailed right past Ephesus. How did Paul manage to see the elders of the Ephesian church to say goodbye to them? Where and how did this take place? (5A.11 and 12)

g) The description of Paul's farewell words to the Ephesian elders gives us a much deeper insight into Paul's ministry in Ephesus. What are some of the things we learn from this? (1B.5 to 7; 5A.13 to 15)

14. Palestine Again: Caesarea (5B.5 and 6A.7)

a) From there they traveled on to Palestine (see map above 5B.1). In which important city did a prophet forewarn Paul in the Spirit not to go up to Jerusalem because persecution awaited him there? (5B.5)

b) What was the name of this prophet? (5B.5)

c) Name one of the leaders of the church in this city. (5B.5)

d) However, Paul insisted on going up to Jerusalem. How long was it before he was back in this city, but in chains, just as the prophet had foretold? (6A.7)

15. Jerusalem Again (Lesson 5B)

a) What was it that Paul hoped would heal the breach between the Jewish and Gentile Christians? (5B.6)

b) Instead, what did the Jewish Christians push Paul into doing, that seemed so contrary to all his previous teaching? (5B.7)

c) Alas! It certainly didn't achieve its purpose. What did the Jews do instead? (5B.8)

d) Who saved Paul from the wrath of the Jews? (5B.8)

e) How did Paul avoid being beaten harshly? (5B.10)

f) When he was sent before the Jewish Sanhedrin what did the high priest order someone to do to Paul? (5B.12)

g) How did Paul split the Sanhedrin into two contending parties? (5B.13)

h) The Jews then plotted to kill Paul. Who thwarted this plot? (6A.2 and 3)

i) Where did the Roman captain send Paul, under heavy military escort, in order to secure his life? (6A.4)

Now review Part 2, before going on.

Part 3: A Prisoner in Caesarea, Malta and Rome

16. Back in Caesarea: But as a Prisoner (Lesson 6A)

As the prophet Agabus had foretold, Paul was bound in Jerusalem, and was back in Caesarea as a prisoner within two weeks.

a) Who was one of the leaders of the church in Caesarea? (6A.8)

b) What members of his family also ministered there? (6A.8)

c) Paul was able to witness before three important authorities in Caesarea. What were their names and those of their wives? Which of them were Gentiles and which Jewish? (6A.11)

d) Reading between the lines of history, Luke must have been actively engaged in some very important work during these two years in Caesarea. What work? (6A.20 to 24 and map)

e) From here Paul was sent on to Rome. Why? (6A.14)

17. Journey to Rome (See Map above 6B.1)

a) Paul was accompanied by two of his most faithful friends on this journey. Name them. (6B.2)

b) Name the Roman captain in charge of the prisoners. (6B.1)

c) On which island did they dock? What did Paul counsel? What did the others decide to do? What was the result? (6B.5 to 7)

d) Give 3 or 4 events that showed how Paul the prisoner was really the moral leader on this voyage. (6B.12)

e)   Where were they all washed up eventually, safe and sound? (6B.10)

f)   In 1864, a Scotsman by the name of James Smith, proved the total accuracy of Luke's account of this voyage. How did he do this? (6B.11)

g)   What miracles did Paul do on this island? (6B.13)

h)   What events greatly encouraged Paul as they walked the last stage of the journey in their approach to Rome? (6B.15)

18. First Imprisonment in Rome (Lesson 7A)

a)   Under what conditions was Paul in this first imprisonment in Rome? (7A.1)

b)   What different ministries was he able to perform? (7A.1 – Teacher bubble)

c)   Name some of those he was able to help at this time? (7A.4 to 7)

d)   What are the letters that he probably wrote at this time? (7A.19)

e)   Name one or two of the things that Paul found to **rejoice about** even though he was a prisoner. In which of his prison letters do we find these things? (6C.2 and 3)

19. Between Imprisonments (7B.1 to 8)

a)   What places must Paul have visited during this new period of freedom? (7B.3)

b)   What two letters did he write at this time? To whom? Where was each of the people to whom he wrote at this time? (7B.2 and 5 to 8)

c)   What new country may he have visited at this time? What evidence is there of this? (7B.4)

20. Second Imprisonment in Rome and Death (7B.9 to 11)

a)   Under what very different conditions was Paul a prisoner this time? (7B.9)

b)   What letter did Paul write at this time? (7B.10)

c)   Who was the Roman Emperor at this time? (7B.9 and 10)

d)   What atrocities had he committed against the Christians? (7B.9)

e)   In spite of this, what did Paul do at his trial? (7B.10)

f)   Who alone stood by Paul at his trial? (7B.10)

g)   What kind of death did Paul probably suffer? (7B.11)

h)   How do we know he was completely without fear at the time? Find some references to show this from his letters. (7B.11)

i)   Far from being afraid, how did Paul view the prospect of dying for his faith in Christ? Find references to show this from the letters he wrote at the time. (7B.11)

j)   What were the principal things that Paul was still looking forward to, even as an old man, suffering the most terrible indignities, and facing death at any moment? (Lesson 7C).

21. Finding Places on the Map

Which letters mark the following places on the Test Map (page 155)? In each case you can find the place on the **Maps** in the Lesson references given.

a)	Achaia [province]	(1A.1, Map B)
b)	Asia [province]	(1A.1)
c)	Caesarea	(6B.1)
d)	Colossae	(2A.5)
e)	Corinth	(3A.17)
f)	Crete	(6B.1)
g)	Ephesus	(1A.1)
h)	Galatia [province]	(1A.1, Map A)
i)	Illyricum [province]	(4A.1)
j)	Jerusalem	(5B.1)
k)	Macedonia [province]	(4A.1)
l)	Malta	(6B.1)
m)	Miletus	(5A.10)
n)	Philippi	(3A.17)
o)	Rome	(6B.1)
p)	Troas	(3A.17)

Try and think of the principal events that happened in each of these places.

22. Paul's Letters

Review the main teaching points of each of Paul's letters as summarized in the chart in Lesson 8B, starting on the next page, as well as the order in which the letters were written.

Lesson 8B
Index: Paul's Letters – Review Chart

Chapters shown in parentheses; Lessons in square brackets

Letters from Ephesus, Macedonia and Corinth		
1. 1 Corinthians (From Ephesus to Corinth) [2B.19 to 29]		
Pastoral advice on		
• Divisions (1–4)	• Pay for pastors (9)	
• Immorality (5)	• Holy Communion (10–11)	
• Heathen courts (6)	• Spiritual gifts (12–14)	
• Marriage (7)	• Resurrection (15)	
• Food offered to idols (8)	• Christian aid (16)	
2. 2 Corinthians (From Macedonia to Corinth)		
God's Strength in Weakness		
• *"Treasure in jars of clay"*	(2 Cor. 4:7)	[3C.6]
• *"Captives in Christ's victory procession"*	(2 Cor. 2:14–16)	[3C.9]
3. Romans (From Corinth to Rome)		
Put right with God by faith	(Rom. 1:17)	[4A.10]
Righteousness		
• needed	(Rom. 1 to 3)	
• imputed	(Rom. 4 and 5)	
• imparted	(Rom. 6 to 8)	[Analysis – 4B.27]
Jew/Gentile relationship	(Rom. 9 to 11)	[5C]
Continuous evangelism and training	(Rom. 10)	[4C]
Mission to Spain	(Rom. 15:24, 28)	[4A.3 to 5]

From Rome (1st. Imprisonment) to Ephesus, Colossae, Philemon and Philippi:

4. Ephesians

The Holy Spirit as

• a seal	(Eph. 1:13)	[1C.9]
• a guarantee	(Eph. 1:14)	[1C.10]
• power	(Eph. 1:17–20)	[1C.11]

5. Colossians

Problems and solutions:		[2C.6 and 8]
• Deceptive philosophy	(Col. 2:8)	
• Human commands	(Col. 2:22)	
• Unspiritual mind	(Col. 2:18)	
• Earthly nature	(Col. 3:5)	

6. Philemon

Onesimus converted in Rome: returns to Philemon in Colossae

	(Phm. vv.10–12)	[7A.6 and 7]

7. Philippians

Joy in union with Christ	(Phil. 3:1; 4:4)	[6C.3]

Between Imprisonments to Timothy and Titus:

8. 1 Timothy

(In Ephesus)	(1 Tim. 1:2–3)

9. Titus

(In Crete)

Leadership training	(Titus 1:4–5)	[7B.5 to 8]

From Rome (2nd. Imprisonment) to Timothy:

10. 2 Timothy

(In Ephesus)

Still looking forward	(2 Tim. 4:6–8)	[7C.1]

Supplement 1
Paul's Letters

Period in Paul's Ministry	Order of Writing	Letter Written		Paul's Approx. Age
		To:	From:	
First Missionary Journey	1	GALATIA	ANTIOCH (in Syria) On returning from Galatia	49
Second Missionary Journey	2	THESSALONICA (first letter)	CORINTH	51
	3	THESSALONICA (second letter)		52
Third Missionary Journey	4	CORINTH (first letter)	EPHESUS	56
	5	CORINTH (second letter)	MACEDONIA (return visit)	56
	6	ROME	CORINTH (return visit)	57
First Imprisonment	7	EPHESUS	ROME (probably)	61–62
	8	COLOSSAE		
	9	PHILEMON (in Colossae)		
	10	PHILIPPI		
Period when released	11	TITUS (in Crete)	MACEDONIA (probably	63–66
	12	TIMOTHY (in Ephesus) (first letter)		
Second Imprisonment and Martyrdom	13	TIMOTHY (in Ephesus) (second letter)	ROME (probably)	67

Note: Paul's age is calculated here as if he were born in the year 1 A.D. (which can't be far from the mark). Therefore his age at any time corresponds to the date A.D.
These ages (and dates) are, of course, only tentative, but they do give a good general idea of Paul's age at the time of writing.

Supplement 2
Paul's Visits and Letters to Corinth

1.	**First visit to Corinth**	**SECOND MISSIONARY JOURNEY** On second Missionary Journey. Church set up in home of Gaius Titius Justus. (Acts 18:1, 7; compare Romans 16:23)
2.	**Letter No.1**	**THIRD MISSIONARY JOURNEY (EPHESUS)** (Now lost) called "previous" letter, written from Ephesus to Corinth about danger of mixing with immoral people.　　(See 1 Cor. 5:9) **Note:** This was followed by the Corinthians writing a letter to Paul with a number of queries. Brought to Paul by Stephanas, Fortunatus and Achaicus.　　(1 Cor. 16:17)
3.	**Letter No.2**	Our **1 Corinthians** in the New Testament written from Ephesus (see 1 Cor. 16:8 and compare with 16:19) on learning from Chloe's family of divisions in Corinth (see 1 Cor. 1:11) and in answer to letter of queries brought from Corinth by Stephanas, Fortunatus and Achaicus.　　(1 Cor. 16:17 and 1 Cor. 7:1)
4.	**Second Visit to Corinth**	(Not recorded in Acts, but see 2 Cor. 13:2). Called **"painful"** visit.　　(See 2 Cor. 2:1)
5.	**Letter No.3**	(Now lost) called **"severe"** letter, sent from Ephesus with Titus, with sharp criticism of disorders in church.　　(See 2 Cor. 2:4; 7:8)
6.	**Letter No.4**	**(MACEDONIA)** (Our **2 Corinthians** in the new testament) written from Macedonia (almost certainly Philippi) to Corinth (see Acts 20:1), to say how glad he was to receive news from Titus that they were sorry for all the disorders. Titus returned to Corinth with this letter. (2 Cor. 7:6–7)
7.	**Third visit to Corinth**	**(ACHAIA – CORINTH)** (Acts 20:2. Announced in 2 Cor. 12:14 and 13:1) To Corinth. On this **three** month visit Paul wrote **Romans** (as we shall see).

Supplement 3
Mission to Asia

(New Testament books or passages bearing on Paul's mission to Asia and its results.)

	REFERENCE	ITS RELEVANCE	EXTRA NOTES
1	Acts 16.6	Paul's early desire to evangelize Asia; prevented at the time by the Holy Spirit.	At the time (second missionary journey) God had other plans: • meet up with Luke in Troas. • Paul's vision of Macedonian man in Troas.
2	Acts 18:18–21	On returning from his second missionary journey Paul called in at Ephesus and left Priscilla and Aquila there.	Paul then returned to Jerusalem and Antioch before launching out on the third journey.
3	Acts 18:24–27	Meanwhile Priscilla and Aquila instructed Apollos in Ephesus.	Apollos went to Corinth before Paul returned to Ephesus.
4	Acts 19:1–41	Tells of Paul's Mission to Asia. (Acts 19:10)	This lasted over 2 years, and ALL Asia heard the message.
5	1 Corinthians	Letter written **FROM Ephesus** in Asia. (1 Cor. 16:8; 15:32)	Some think that Paul had to fight lions in Ephesus (1 Cor. 15:32). However, this is probably metaphorical.
6	2 Corinthians	Written just after Paul left Asia, but refers back to his stay there. (2 Cor. 1:8)	Opposition to Paul in Ephesus grew so strong that he left under dire threat to his life. We learn this from 2 Corinthians which he wrote just after this.
7	Acts 20:17–38	From Paul's farewell to the Ephesian elders we can learn more about what he did when he was in Ephesus.	From this we see that Paul foresaw how false teachers would damage the church in Ephesus.
8	a) Ephesians b) Colossians c) Philemon	Paul's letters **TO Asia** from prison (probably in Rome).	a) Probably a circular letter to several Asian churches. b) Colossae was another of the Asian churches. c) Philemon, a rich slave owner, was a member of the church in Colossae.
9	a) 1 Timothy b) 2 Timothy	a) Written **TO Timothy** who was in Asia. (1 Tim. 1:3) b) Timothy was probably still in Ephesus. (2 Tim. 15, 18)	
10	Revelation	Written by John (probably the Apostle) **TO 7 churches in Asia**. (Rev. 1:4, 11 and 2:1)	The longest of the New Testament documents written to Asia. Probably much later and so reveals state of churches after some time.

TESTS

Note: The Test Map is used throughout the Tests and can be found on the last page of this book.

TEST 1A

1. a)   On his way out on his third journey Paul once again visited the home town of Timothy and the other churches in the province of Galatia. In what way did these churches decide to help Paul?

    _____

    b)   Which letter marks the province of Galatia on the Test Map (on the last page of this book)?   Letter _____

2. a)   Before Paul got back to Ephesus, what new Christian had arrived there who had to be taught more exactly the word of the Lord?   _____

    b)   Who were especially responsible for teaching him?   _____

    c)   What baptism had this new Christian been teaching? _____

    d)   To which city did this man go, just before Paul arrived back in Ephesus?_____

    e)   What sad side effect did this bring there?   _____

    f)   In which city had this man been born?   _____

    g)   And in which continent?   _____

    h)   What was his nationality?   _____

3. On the Test Map (last page) which letter marks

    a)   the province of Asia?   Letter _____

    b)   Ephesus? (Follow the journey lines carefully)   Letter _____

TEST 1B

1. a)   Now at last Paul was able to achieve his long ambition, and witness for Christ in Asia. In which big city did he set up his base?   _____

    b)   Which letter marks it on the Test Map?   Letter _____

2. What huge temple, one of the Seven Wonders of the World, adorned this beautiful city?   _____

3. a)   How did Paul support himself in this city?   _____

    b)   Whom would he have joined in this work?   _____

    c)   Apart from keeping himself and his companions, what else did they do with their earnings?   _____

4. We know that Paul was careful to teach the whole purpose of God. In which two types of place did he teach in this city?

    _____ and _____

5. When he first arrived in Asia, Paul found a small group of believers.

    a) About how many were they?   _____

    b) Like Apollos when he first arrived in Asia, what
        was the only baptism these disciples knew about? _____

    c) What other very important truth had they never heard about? _____

6. a) In whose name did Paul then baptize them?   _____

    b) What else did Paul do to them?   _____

    c) Who descended on them at this moment?   _____

    d) What two things did they then do?

        _____ and _____

7. When Paul wrote to these Christians later what did he urge them

    a) **not** to do to the Holy Spirit?   _____

    b) to **do** with the Holy Spirit?   _____

TEST 1C

1. In Ephesians Paul gives three illustrations to teach us more about the Holy Spirit. Which of these illustrations shows us (in each case give the Bible reference) how the Holy Spirit

    a) marks a Christian as belonging to God?

        _____   _____

    b) is a kind of down payment assuring us that one day we will enter fully into the wonderful inheritance God has in store for us?

        _____   _____

    c) can change a Christian completely and one day will raise him from the dead?

        _____   _____

2. Name any two of the important things that Paul says in Ephesians should reveal the presence of the Holy Spirit in our lives, with the Bible references.

    _____   _____

    _____   _____

TEST 2A

1. Where did Paul preach and teach about the
Kingdom of God, during his first three months in Ephesus? _____

2. Then, as in every other city, the unbelieving Jews made things so difficult that Paul withdrew.

    a) Where in Ephesus did he go to teach, instead? _____

    b) How long did he continue this? _____

    c) How far did the message spread during this time? _____

3. a) Which three other churches came into being while Paul was ministering in Ephesus?

    _____ _____ _____

    b) Which of these received a letter from Paul

    1) that has been preserved in the New Testament? _____

    2) that has **not** been preserved for us in the New Testament? _____

4. a) What wealthy slave owner from Colossae was
converted through Paul's ministry, probably in Ephesus? _____

    b) What letter marks his home town of Colossae on the Test Map? Letter _____

5. a) What two kinds of miracle did Paul do in Ephesus?

    _____ _____

    b) What are two of Paul's belongings that were
used on some of these occasions to heal people? _____

6. a) Who tried to imitate Paul's miracles by casting
out evil spirits? _____

    b) What did the man with the evil spirit do? _____

    c) How did he leave them? _____

7. This really shook up the Christians in Ephesus.

    a) What kind of books did they begin to burn as a result of this? _____

    b) What was the value of all these books? _____

8. What name do we give to the letter that Paul wrote
to the Corinthians and that has been lost? _____

TEST 2B

1. a) Now Paul began to make plans for leaving
   Ephesus. Whom did he send ahead of him, with
   Erastus, to Macedonia? _____

   b) After going himself to Macedonia and Achaia, Paul hoped to go on to two cities.

   Which were these? _____ and _____

2. Now Paul's enemies stirred up persecution against him.

   Which two of Paul's friends actually risked their
   lives to save him from death? _____

3. While Paul was passing through this terrible period of tribulation, he suddenly received
   news that divisions and strife had broken out in the church in Corinth.

   a) Who brought this bad news to Ephesus? _____

   b) After which four people were these contending parties named?

   _____ _____ _____ _____

4. a) Which of Paul's letters did he write to try to
   correct these divisions? _____

   b) In which verse of this letter can we see that he
   wrote it from Ephesus? _____

5. Apart from the divisions in the church which Paul deals with in **1 Corinthians 1**, there were a
   number of other grave problems that Paul tried to clear up in 1 Corinthians. For example:

   a) in **1 Corinthians 5** he rebukes the man who had committed a terrible sex sin.
   With whom had this man been sleeping? _____

   b) in **1 Corinthians 6** he rebukes the conflict between Christians.
   Before whom had they been taking these
   disputes to seek a judgment? _____

   c) in **1 Corinthians 7** Paul answers a question the Corinthians had written to ask him about.
   What was this? _____

   d) in **1 Corinthians 8** Paul deals with the problem of the meat the Christians had to buy in
   the markets.
   What kind of meat was this? _____

   e) in **1 Corinthians 9** Some were saying Paul was a second class apostle because he worked
   in a secular job.
   What did Paul refuse to take that led to this accusation? _____

(Continued on next page)

TEST 2B – Continued

f) in **1 Corinthians 10** Paul deals with problems arising in one of the main church services. Which one? _____

g) in **1 Corinthians 11** Paul condemns certain excesses they were committing in the Lord's Supper.
What were they? _____

h) in **1 Corinthians 12, 13** and **14** Paul had to correct the abuse of certain gifts in the church. What kind of gifts? _____

i) in **1 Corinthians 15** Paul had to correct some who were denying a very important truth. What was that truth? _____

TEST 2C

1. In whose house in Colossae did the church meet? _____

2. a) Name the evangelist who established the church there. _____

   b) In which other two churches in Asia did he minister?

   _____ and _____

3. Review the references and your notes in the chart below. Add any new ideas you may have.

Problems in Colossae and Paul's Solutions to them

	Reference in Colossians	Problems	Today's Problems
1)	2:8		
2)	2:16–17 2:20b–23		
3)	2:18		
4)	3:5		
		Solution to our Problems	
1)	2:9–10		
2)	2:13–15		
3)	2:19b–20a		
4)	3:8–10		

TEST 3A

1. While still in Ephesus Paul learned of a grave worsening of the situation in Corinth and so he made a quick second visit to Corinth (which is not recorded in the Acts). What is this visit usually called?

   ☐ a. His "painful" visit.   ☐ b. His "happy" visit.   ☐ c. His "teaching" visit.

2. As things went from bad to worse in Corinth, Paul (still in Ephesus) wrote a sharp letter of rebuke which, like the one we saw in Lesson 2A, called the "previous" letter, is not in the New Testament because it has been lost.

   Who carried this "severe" letter to Corinth for Paul? _____

3. Suddenly trouble blew up in Ephesus.

   a) What was the name of the silversmith who stirred up a riot against Paul? _____

   b) He used to get large gains by making silver models of the temple of the patron goddess of Ephesus.
      What was the name of this goddess? _____

   c) What had happened to his trade as a result of so many people becoming Christians through Paul's ministry? _____

4. This silversmith was so enraged with Paul that he stirred the mob to riot.

   What was the name of Paul's convert from Thessalonica who was dragged into the theatre with Gaius? _____

5. a) What slogan did the mob keep chanting? _____

   b) What did Paul want to do? _____

   c) What did the other believers do? _____

6. a) How long did the mob keep up the chanting? _____

   b) Who eventually got the mob under control and sent the people home? _____

7. So Paul decided to leave Ephesus.

   a) Where did Paul wait in vain for Titus? _____

   b) Where did Paul eventually go to wait for him? _____

8. On the Test Map, which letter marks the position of

   a) Ephesus? _____   b) Troas? _____   c) Philippi? _____   d) Corinth? _____

TEST 3B

1. a) Where did Paul wait in vain for Titus?   _____

    b) In which province did Titus eventually meet Paul?   _____

    c) Which letter marks this province on the Test Map?   Letter _____

    d) Name another member of the missionary team
        that Paul met here, after 6 years of separation.   _____

2. a) From Macedonia Paul launched a major evangelistic outreach, before going on to Corinth
        (Achaia).

        Into which other province (our modern Albania)
        did he reach, according to what he says in Romans?   _____

    b) Which letter marks this province on the Test Map?   Letter _____

3. a) Where did Paul write 2 Corinthians?   _____

    b) Who carried it to Corinth for him?   _____

    c) In which province was Corinth?   _____

    d) Which letter marks this province on the Test Map?   Letter _____

4. The following list includes six of the main reasons Paul had in sending 2 Corinthians. Which
    are they? (Check the correct boxes)

    ☐ a) To explain why he had changed his plans to visit them to those who were calling him
           fickle.

    ☐ b) To ask them to get on with collecting their help for Jerusalem so that they would
           have it ready when he arrived.

    ☐ c) To congratulate them because they already had their help for Jerusalem all gathered
           in.

    ☐ d) To urge them to punish still further the man who had committed an awful sin.

    ☐ e) To ask them to forgive this man now that he had repented.

    ☐ f) To condemn a small group of false apostles who were still undermining Paul's
           authority as a true apostle.

    ☐ g) To congratulate them because there no longer existed any opposition to the truth in
           Corinth.

    ☐ h) To rejoice with them at the incredible success that Titus had in his mission to them.

    ☐ i) To tell them he wouldn't be able to visit them again.

    ☐ j) To tell them he hoped to visit them again soon, which would be his third visit.

TEST 3C

To each answer add the reference in 2 Corinthians from your marked Bible.

1. What did Paul say in 2 Corinthians about his recent sufferings in Asia that express how desperate they were?

   _____   _____

2. Describe the **two** illustrations that Paul gives in this same letter to show how, for the Christian, God's strength is channelled through **weakness**. The pictures in Lesson 3C.6e) and 9 will help.

   _____   _____

   _____   _____

3. Give one of Paul's examples from 2 Corinthians to show the practical outworking of this basic truth.

   _____   _____

TEST 4A

1. a) To which city did Paul now go, once he had finished his work in Macedonia and Illyricum?   _____

   b) In which province was this city?   _____

   c) How long did Paul stay there this time?   _____

   d) Which important letter did he write while he was there?   _____

   e) In whose house was he staying when he wrote this letter?   _____

   f) About how old was Paul when he wrote this letter?   _____

   g) On which of his three missionary journeys did he write this letter?   _____

   h) What was the name of the lady who carried the letter to its destination for him?   _____

   i) What was the name of her home town?   _____

2. Name the following places and give the letter of each on the Test Map.

   a) The city to which he wrote a letter to ask them to become his base (or new Antioch) from which to launch his new missionary journeys west.   _____ _____

   b) The city from which Paul wrote this important letter?   _____ _____

(Continued on next page)

TEST 4A – Continued

    c)   The city to the east that he hoped to visit first to
         deliver aid, before launching out to evangelize the west. _____ _____

3.   Name the country to the far west that Paul hoped to evangelize then.   _____

4.   a)   To which two important groups of Christians, did Paul especially direct his teaching in his letter to the Romans?

                                  _____ and _____

    b)   What was the central doctrine that he applies so powerfully to these two groups of people throughout the letter to the Romans?

         _____

5.   In which chapter in Romans can we learn

    a)   that Paul had lots of friends and converts already
         in Rome (because in this chapter he greets them by name).   Chapter _____

    b)   the text in Habakkuk, which gives us the basic
         theme of this letter: "How a sinner can be put right with God by faith".   Chapter _____

    c)   that Paul hoped the church in Rome would
         provide him with a new base from which to
         launch his new missionary journey to evangelize Spain.   Chapter _____

6.   a)   To what married couple, old friends of Paul's
         who had just moved to Rome from Ephesus,
         did Paul send greetings in his letter to the Romans? _____

    b)   Were they Jews or Gentiles?   _____

TEST 4B (Romans, chapters 1 to 8)

1.   In **Romans, chapters 1, 2 and 3** Paul argues strongly that **all** people, both Jews and Gentiles, are sinners and therefore **need** God's righteousness. In which of these three chapters does Paul especially describe the sins of

    a)   both Jews and Gentiles?   Chapter _____

    b)   the Gentiles alone?   Chapter _____

    c)   the Jews alone?   Chapter _____

2. In **Romans 4 and 5** Paul tells how God **imputes** the righteousness of Christ to all sinners who put their faith in Christ. He uses two people as examples. Which of these does he use

    a) as a **likeness**, in chapter 4?　　　　　　　　　　_____

    b) as a **contrast**, in chapter 5?　　　　　　　　　　_____

3. In **Romans 6, 7 and 8** Paul tells how God imparts the righteousness of Christ to all believers. What examples does he give to explain this in

    a) chapter 6?　　　_____ and _____

    b) chapter 7?　　　　　　　　　　　　　_____

4. Which are the chapters in Romans that mainly deal with **righteousness** being

    a) **needed**?　　　　　　　　　Chapters _____, _____ and _____

    b) **imputed**?　　　　　　　　Chapters _____ and _____

    c) **imparted**?　　　　　　　Chapters _____, _____ and _____

TEST 4C

1. In which chapter in Romans does Paul make his earnest appeal to Christians to **GO** with the gospel to where the people are?　Chapter _____

2. a) What are the two essential parts of Paul's ministry of evangelism that must be carried out **continuously** if there is to be real church growth? In each case give the example from agriculture that Paul uses to make his meaning clear.

    Continuous _____ – _____

    Continuous _____ – _____

    b) In which chapter and verse in 1 Corinthians does Paul teach these two principles of evangelism?　　　　_____

    c) In which chapter and verses in Matthew's Gospel does Jesus command us to do these same two things?　　_____

3. From a practical point of view, what are the two resources that are provided by SEAN which could be used

    a) in the first of the above ministries? _____

    b) in the second of the above ministries?　　_____

TEST 5A

1. After his three months in Corinth, where he wrote his letter to the Romans, Paul intended to go directly to Syria.

    a) To which town in Macedonia did he go instead? _____

    b) Who rejoined the missionary team in this town? _____

    c) What had caused Paul to make this change in plans? _____

    d) What group of people went with him?

    _____

2. From Macedonia, they went across to Troas.

    a) What letter marks it on the Test Map? Letter _____

    b) When they were in Troas, a young man there was killed. How?

    _____

    c) What miracle did Paul do? _____

3. From Troas they went on to Miletus. What letter marks it on the Test Map? Letter _____

4. a) What unusual thing did Paul do on the first leg of his journey?

    _____

    b) What was he probably seeking guidance about at this time?

    _____

5. They sailed right past Ephesus because Paul was in a hurry to reach Jerusalem in time for the feast of Pentecost.

    a) Who came to Miletus to see him from Ephesus? _____

    b) Which letter marks Ephesus on the Test Map? Letter _____

    c) What future danger did Paul warn them against? _____

TEST 5B

1. a) The boat docked seven days in Tyre. What did the believers there tell Paul not to do? _____

    b) In whose power did they speak these words? _____

2. a)   In which port did they finally disembark?   _____

    b)   What letter marks it on the Test Map?   Letter _____

    c)   In whose house did they stay?   _____

    d)   Which of his family spoke God's Word?   _____

    e)   What was the name of the prophet who
         warned Paul what would happen in Jerusalem?   _____

    f)   What did he do to himself to impress his message upon Paul?

         _____

    g)   How did Paul answer him?

         _____

3. a)   What did James ask Paul to offer up in the
         temple to disprove to the Jews the false rumors
         about Paul's preaching and teaching?   _____

    b)   What did the Jews nearly do to Paul, in spite of this?   _____

    c)   Who stopped them, just in time?   _____

    d)   What letter marks Jerusalem on the Test Map?   Letter _____

4. The Roman guard passed Paul over the heads of the raging mob until they got him safely
    to the steps leading into the Roman tower of Antonia which overlooked the temple at that
    time. From here the Roman commander allowed Paul to speak to the Jews.

    a)   In which language did he address them?   _____

    b)   What immediate result did this have on the mob?   _____

    c)   What stopped them listening to him?   _____

5. What did Paul claim to be that saved him from
    being tortured by whipping?   _____

6. a)   Before which council did the Roman
         commander make Paul stand on the following day?   _____

    b)   Into which two groups were the members of this council divided?

         _____ and _____

    c)   To which group did the high priest belong?   _____

    d)   What did he order someone to do to Paul?   _____

    e)   What great truth did Paul preach about that
         caused the two groups in the Council to fight each other?   _____

(Continued on next page)

TEST 5B – Continued

    f)   Which group believed in this truth?   _____

    g)   Which did not?   _____

    h)   Who got Paul out of the pandemonium?   _____

7.   a)   With whom did Paul meet that same night?   _____

    b)   Where did he say Paul would have to go as his witness?   _____

    c)   The stark contrast between the Lord Jesus, the spiritual high priest, and the brute who had just ordered Paul to be struck on the mouth, must have impressed Paul.

        To Paul, who was the perfect high priest?   _____

    d)   In which book in the New Testament is this idea clearly expressed?   _____

TEST 5C

1.   a)   What is the main theme that runs throughout Romans 9 to 11?

    b)   What command of Jesus does Paul show he has obeyed in these chapters, in his relationship to the Jews?   _____

2.   What kind of craftsman does Paul use in **Romans 9** to illustrate God's sovereignty?   _____

3.   What does Paul urge Christians to do in **Romans 10**?_____

4.   In Paul's illustration of the cultivated and the wild olive trees, who were represented by each of the following?

    a)   The cultivated olive tree.   _____

    b)   The wild olive tree.   _____

    c)   The broken off branches of the cultivated olive tree.   _____

    d)   The branches of the wild olive tree grafted into the cultivated olive tree.   _____

    e)   The broken off branches of the cultivated olive tree grafted back.   _____

TEST 6A

1. a) About how many Jewish conspirators plotted to assassinate Paul? _____

   b) Who leaked the plot to Paul so he could tell Lysias, the Roman commander? _____

   c) To which city on the coast did Lysias send Paul under heavy military escort? _____

   d) What letter marks it on the Test Map? Letter _____

   e) Name a church leader in this city. _____

   f) Name the prophet who, in this city, foretold that Paul would be bound if he went to Jerusalem. _____

   g) How long after this prophecy did Paul return to this city from Jerusalem as a prisoner? _____

   h) How long was Paul kept a prisoner in this city? _____

2. Name the three authorities (and their women, when applicable) before whom Paul witnessed in Caesarea.

   a) _____ and his wife _____

   b) _____

   c) _____ and his sister _____

3. Of the five people (named in No.2) say which of them

   a) were Romans. _____

   b) were half-Jewish. _____

   c) was really shaken, and afraid, when Paul preached about goodness, self-control and the coming Day of Judgment. _____

   d) was the judge before whom Tertullus accused Paul on behalf of Ananias, the high priest. _____

   e) was the one to whom Paul made his appeal to the Emperor, Caesar. _____

   f) shouted that Paul was mad. _____

   g) sneered at Paul for trying to make him a Christian. _____

4. Name the two different kinds of ministry that went on during Paul's stay in Caesarea.

   _____

   _____

TEST 6B

1. Name the Roman officer who was in charge of Paul on the journey to Rome. _____

2. Name Paul's two traveling companions on this journey.

   _____ and _____

3. a) On which island was "Fair Havens" situated? _____

   b) What letter marks it on the Test Map? Letter _____

   c) What happened after they left there? _____

   d) What Jewish celebration had just passed? _____

4. In what ways did Paul contribute to the success of this voyage, before the ship broke up? Give any three of these.

   _____

   _____

   _____

5. a) On what island were they shipwrecked? _____

   b) What letter marks it on the Test Map? Letter _____

   c) How many days after leaving Crete did this happen? _____

   d) Name the Scotsman who reenacted this voyage in the year 1854 thus proving Luke's incredible accuracy. _____

6. a) Name the chief official on this island who received Paul and the others so kindly. _____

   b) What two miracles does Luke describe in detail that took place there?

   _____

   _____

7. On reaching Italy, what two events must have made a terrific impression on Paul's Roman guards?

   _____

   _____

8. At last they reached Rome! What letter marks it on the Test Map? Letter _____

TEST 6C

1. Give three of the things that Paul was able to rejoice about, when he was in prison.

    In each case give the reference from Philippians.   **Reference**

    a) _____   _____

    b) _____   _____

    c) _____   _____

2. In which verses, in Philippians 2, does Paul give us his Christian hymn on Christ?   vv. _____

3. a) To what does Paul compare the Christian life as
        a warning not to keep looking back to our past failures?   _____

    b) Applying this illustration, what attitude did Paul
        take as a corrective to looking back?   _____

    c) Find the reference to this passage.   _____

TEST 7A

1. a) What was the total population of Rome at the time Paul was there?   _____

    b) How long did Paul stay in the city this first time?   _____

    c) Where did he stay?   _____

    d) By whom was he watched day and night?   _____

2. Whom did he invite to see him, only three days
    after his arrival in Rome?   _____

3. Name the visitor Paul had in Rome

    a) whom Paul forgave for having abandoned him
        on the first missionary journey.   _____

    b) who was a slave that Paul brought to faith in
        Christ, and then sent back to his Christian master.   _____

4. a) What was the name of this slave's master, to
        whom Paul also wrote a letter?   _____

    b) Name the town where he lived.   _____

    c) In his letter Paul asked him to receive his slave
        back, no longer as a slave, but as something
        else. What?   _____

(Continued on next page)

TEST 7A – Continued

5. Paul sent envoys from Rome to his other churches. To which of these churches did he send

    a) Timothy?   _____

    b) Tychicus?   _____ and _____

6. According to tradition, which of the following books of the New Testament were written by Paul (and Luke) during this period of house arrest in Rome?

    ☐ a. The Gospel according to Luke

    ☐ b. Ephesians

    ☐ c. The Acts of the Apostles

    ☐ d. Philippians

    ☐ e. 2 Corinthians

    ☐ f. 1 Thessalonians

    ☐ g. Romans

    ☐ h. Philemon

    ☐ i. Colossians

7. Name another letter that Paul wrote at this time which has been lost.   _____

8. What were the four principal aspects of Paul's ministry during his first period of imprisonment in Rome?

    _____   _____

    _____   _____

TEST 7B

1. a) What did Paul ask Philemon to do that showed that he hoped to be released from his first imprisonment?

        _____

    b) When he was released, how many more years of freedom did Paul probably enjoy?   _____

2. Name the two people to whom Paul wrote during this period between his imprisonments. In each case say where they were and give the letter that marks the place on the Test Map.

    To _____ in _____   Letter _____

    To _____ in _____   Letter _____

3. What important new theme do these two letters have in common?

    _____

4. Name two places that Paul visited during the period between his imprisonments.

    _____ and _____

5. a) Name the **last** letter Paul wrote. _____

    b) Where was he at the time and in what city? _____

    c) What happened to him shortly after? _____

6. How did his second imprisonment differ from his first?

    _____

7. a) Who was the Emperor at this time? _____

    b) What atrocity did he commit in the year 64 A.D.? _____

    c) Where did the Christians hide during this time?

        _____

    d) Who was the only one to stand by Paul during his last trials? _____

8. What did Paul proclaim in his trial, that turned the prisoners' dock into a pulpit?

    _____

9. a) By what method of execution did Paul die? _____

    b) What happened to Paul then? _____

BLANK PAGE

TEST MAP

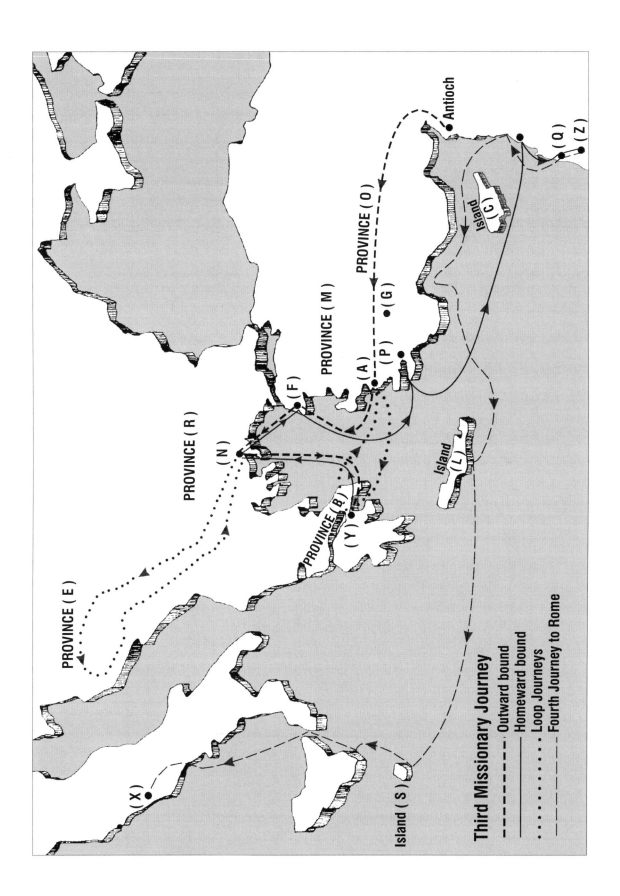

Antioch

(Q) (Z)

PROVINCE (O)

Island (C)

PROVINCE (M)

(A)

(P) • (G)

(F)

PROVINCE (R)

(N)

Island (L)

PROVINCE (B)

(Y)

PROVINCE (E)

Island (S)

(X)

Third Missionary Journey

- - - - Outward bound
——— Homeward bound
· · · · · · Loop Journeys
– – – Fourth Journey to Rome

BLANK PAGE

HAS THIS COURSE BEEN A BLESSING TO YOU?

WOULD YOU LIKE TO BE A BLESSING TO OTHERS?

SEAN is a small missionary organization that reaches out through its courses to more than 100 countries in over 80 languages. Using our materials, national Christians reach areas where foreign missionaries cannot venture.

Please consider now if you would like to help others by praying and supporting our ministry. You can find out more about SEAN International and the courses which are available by visiting our website:

www.seaninternational.org or by email to **contact@seaninternational.org**